CRUISING THE INSIDE PASSAGE TO ALASKA

A practical guide to traveling north by motorboat

Robb Keystone

Copyright © 2012 Robb Keystone

All rights reserved.

DEDICATION

This travel guide is dedicated to all of our friends and fellow cruisers who have traveled with Star Rove and Sea Spirit. May your winds be fair, your eye true, and your love of adventure unbounded.

Special thanks to my lovely wife Mary Frances and daughters Coco and Reisha who let me go off into the great unknown.

PASSAGES:

We have been to Alaska five times. Twice by powerboat (Sea Spirit a 32 foot Mainship) to Sitka and Baranov Hot Springs and 3 times by Sailboat (Star Rover a 44 IORC ocean racer) to Baranov bay and Glacier Bay at the north end of the Inside Passage.

FULL DISCLOSURE:

This book was originally released as "Sailing the Inside Passage to Alaska" If you bought that book you sure don't need this book as it is mostly the same. I have revised the book adding information on AIS. I have changed the pictures high lighting motor vessels instead of sailboats. My thinking is: motor cruisers are not going to be interested in a book on sailing; but they might well benefit form the cruising suggestions and stories in this book. So yes, it is marketing. Mea Culpa. I did cruse on a motorboat (Lobster boat) to Sitka and back. and I mostly motored on my sailboat. There you have it.

WHY GO?

The Inside Passage is one of the best places to travel by trawler in the world. Yes it may be cold, and the wind may be in your face, but you can spend your whole life traveling to and from Glacier Bay and never stay in the same anchorage twice. Once you leave Cape Caution, most travelers you meet are friendly, helpful, and have a spirit of adventure. This is truly God's country.

CONTENTS

Section One: Preparation

Some thoughts on getting ready and being ready

Anchor chain:

Many places to anchor in Alaska are at least 50 feet deep so using a 6 to 1 ratio you need 300 feet of chain. The best choice of chain for medium size boats is 5/16 high test. This chain has about the same strength as 3/8 BBB. The primary reason for using 5/16 is that 300 feet of BBB chain is very hard to bring up. For a windlass we use a 1200 watt Lofran Tigress and it works very well. Also, if you're using a combination of chain and line, I would recommend at least 100 feet of chain so that the chain is heavy enough to lie on the bottom.

Type of anchor:

For our 44-foot boat, we use a plow CQR of about 50 lbs. The anchor has worked well except in conditions of a hard bottom like Friday Harbor. Friends report the new anchors like the Rocna work well in these conditions. Remember to use a swivel and to wire tie the shackle so it doesn't come loose.

To keep the boat from jerking on the anchor, many cruisers use a snubber.

I also use a line with a hook to fasten the chain to the boat once the anchor is deployed.

How to anchor:

Mark the chain every 50 feet with a bright paint mark. We use one mark for 50 feet, two marks for 100 feet, and so on. Look at the depth sounder and add at least three times the depth to the bottom. If there is room, a 6 to 1 fetch is much preferred.

Lower the chain all the way down to the bottom. Back the boat slowly away from the prevailing wind until you have the desired scope. Now vigorously back the boat until she stops dead. If she doesn't stop you're not anchored properly.

How to get the anchor up:

Motor slowly towards the chain until the chain is straight up and the winch starts to groan. Lock the chain. Gun the motor until the anchor breaks free. Go into neutral. Pull up the chain.

Some other anchoring ideas:

In places like Princess Louisa and other fjords the water is very deep, well beyond the length of our chain. We simply let out all our chain, back to shore, and tie to a metal ring or a tree using our floating yellow line. Typically we carry 400 feet of the floating yellow ½ inch line. Sometimes we tie two lines in a V to the shore. Tying to a tree is also useful when you don't want to swing.

Secondary anchors:

We carry a 25-pound Danforth and extra line and a 2nd CQR with 100 feet of chain and 250 feet of 5/8th line. We also have a small anchor for the dinghy and a grappling hook.

Navigation:

Old School: Have everything down below in the navigation area where it is nice and dry and out of the way. For the single-handed sailor, Navstations down below are useless.

New School: Have everything right by the wheel. This includes two chart plotters, radio, and autopilot.

We like two chart plotters for redundancy. We keep one close range at 1 mile and the other at the range of 4 miles. This system has the advantage of showing rocks and buoys at close range and freighters and cruise ships at a distance. Make sure you have the software to go all the way up. I've I had the experience of the chart plotter stopping at Port

Hardy. It's kind of ugly to see a blank screen in the middle of a foggy day.

A basic rule in navigating is that Fear Is Good. We turn 90 degrees away from all ferries, cruise ships, and tugs with barges. Relatively speaking we are standing still to their 20 knots. We turn on the motor if we're not making at least 8 knots to get away from danger. Forget the rules of the road. Forget who has the right of way.   Bigger is meaner and meaner wins. Get out of their way so you can live another day.

An Ipad with a Bad-Elf chip is an excellent choice for a third plotter. Remember to load your charts ahead of time.

http://www.amazon.com/Bad-Elf-Receiver-generation-66-channel/dp/B0035Y7ZJattachment.

Binoculars: just buy the cheapest model of the Steiner. http://www.binoculars.com/binoculars/marine-binoculars/steiner8x30militarymarinebinoculars.cfm.

You won't be sorry.

Radar:

Don't leave home without it. If you cannot see the radar from the helm it's useless. Make sure the radar is set to 2 to 4 miles so you have enough time to heed the warning.

 Some thoughts on radar:

We replaced our Furuno radar with the new Lowrance 3 G digital radar. The digital radar is much easier to see with a white background and red targets. It draws only 1 amp on transmit, instead of 3.5 amps and is not dangerous to stand in front of.

According to the specs for the new radar, "the Lowrance Broadband 3G Radar is highly sensitive, solid state radar for unsurpassed clarity, detection, and separation of targets at close and long ranges. With instant on and a significantly lower power draw, the Lowrance 3G radar makes for an ideal radar unit for sailboats, smaller center consoles, or any other vessels with limited on board power. Broadband radar technology uses a dedicated solid state transmitter and receiver inside the radome to be continually transmitting and listening for different frequency wave lengths for object identification; making the Broadband 3G Radar much safer for use and mounting locations than conventional microwave, pulsed based radars of the past. The use of 2 antennas and continuous wavelength measurement, instead of time based, makes broadband radar produce unparalleled close range performance down to 200 ft. with no dead zone around the vessel while still delivering a range of up to 24 NM."

Fog:

We've had fog so thick we couldn't see the mast! Ship foghorns just scare the hell out of you ;which is a good thing.

Make sure you have an air horn with plenty of canned gas. Even better, have a radio that will automatically send out a blast tone. It gets pretty tiring blowing the air horn every 2 minutes.

Charts:

We recommend the following charts in addition to chart books.

- Discovery Passage Chart 3539

- Yaculta Rapids Chart 3543

- Broughtons Chart 3515 and Chart 3547

- The big chart of Queen Charlotte Sound- Chart 3744

- Venn Passage (Prince Rupert) Chart 3955

- Glacier Bay Chart 17318

- Jackson Passage Chart 3734

Safety:

DSC – Digital Selective Calling

The manual says... "DSC was developed to replace a call in older procedures. Because a DSC signal uses a stable signal with a narrow bandwidth and the receiver has no squelch, it has a slightly longer range than analog signals, with up 25 percent longer range and significantly faster. DSC senders are programmed with the ship's Maritime Mobile Service Identity (MMSI) and may be connected to the ship's Global Positioning System (GPS), which allows the apparatus to know who it is, what time it is and where it is. This allows a distress signal to be sent very quickly. Digital Selective Calling is a capability that enables you to transmit vital information including your boat's identification, position and time of distress using SeaTalk or NEMA 0183 data from you GPS."

Personal Locator Beacon:

A good safety thing to have on you at all times.

http://www.amazon.com/ACR-Aqualink-2882-Personal-Includes/dp/B003BQM058/ref=sr_1_4?ie=UTF8&qid=1346198586&sr=8-4&keywords=personal+locator+beacon

Personal Floatation Device:

We like the belt floats because they're so easy to wear. We use the Revere Comfortmax Inflatable Belt Pack Manual Type III Personal Flotation Device (Red, 30-52-Inch).

AIS: Automatic Identification System

 People are adopting it because it shows where ships are in relation the yachtsman. To quote from their website,

"AIS is initially intended to help ships avoid collisions, as well as assisting port authorities to better control sea traffic. AIS transponders on board vessels include a GPS (Global Positioning System) receiver, which collects position and movement details. It includes also a VHF transmitter, which transmits periodically this information on two VHF channels (frequencies 161.975 MHz and 162.025 MHz – old VHF channels 87 & 88) and makes this data available to the public domain. Other vessels or base stations are able to receive this information, process it using special software and display vessels locations on a chart plotter or on a computer."

We are partial to the Standard Horizon Gx2200B with AIS,AIS SART target display. DSC calling, GPS compass display speaker mike 30 W PA hailer/fog. AIS identifies the target speed and heading of the vessels around you. The targets are identified on the screen and AIs can be outputted to the chart plotter. DSC calling enables you to call a specific boat like a phone number. The fog horn is electric so you don't have to blow the silly horn till you get blue in the face or run out of canned air .To activate AIS you need to apply for an NMNI number from boat.us or from the government web site. Boat .us numbers are much easier to get. The government site is a bit convoluted. Word has it that boat.us numbers do not work in Canada. There is also a caution to input the AIS number you receive correctly. If you get it wrong you will have to take your radio to a dealer. In short get the radio with AIS working before you leave! We also recommend you order the 8 inch PA horn Speaker for the foghorn. Amazon has the 2200B for $324. The speaker is $43.

http://www.marinetraffic.com/ais/

Auto Pilot:

We went four times to Alaska and British Columbia without. This trip we had a CPT autopilot and found it delightful. That said…the biggest danger of an autopilot is lack of attention to logs and lobster pots .After 7 hours running on autopilot I kiss the steering wheel, so much less fatigue than manual. Nowadays, B&G, Simrad, Raetheon all make excellent autopilots. Some pilots have issues running true north so ask if there are any issues.

Thrusters; There are few things more unpleasant than being in a quiet an harbor and hearing a power boat come in and immediately begin using thrusters in the middle of the channel. If your cruiser has two motors practice one forward and one in reverse to swing the boat. If you have one screw practice the tugboat maneuver for getting away from the dock. Tie bow to dock and nudge boat forward. She will swing out or in depending on prop walk. In forward she swings one way, in reverse she swings the other. After you try all these suggestions then use the thruster as Gods gift. Wonderful but we can do without.

Fishing:

Manual vs. electric down riggers:

We bought a Canon electric down rigger two years ago and found it splendid for hauling up and down the 12-pound lead ball used for salmon fishing. We generally fish at 3 to 4 knots. We look for a mound about 80 feet and fish at slack tide about 20 feet off the top of the mound. We also fish where there are strong currents and depth changes like the mouth of inlets and rivers. The electric rigger is perfect because you can set the depth easily. We use mostly green flashers but we vary the color as some days the fish only hit one color.

Nets:

Forget getting the fish out of the water without a net. The best one we have seen is a telescoping/folding net we bought at Cabela's. http://www.cabelas.com/ Item: IK-312740. It extends by pulling on the handle. You need at least a 6-foot net to get the fish out of the water. We pour a bit of vodka into the gills to kill the fish.

Crab pots.

We like the metal ones. Make sure the gate swings easily and the bait is firmly tied to the bottom. We use fish heads, cat food or chicken. Normally the crab pot floats are sold in red and white. Change the color with a can of spray paint so the color is unique.

Learn the difference between male and female crabs. The female crabs are not taken. You also need a gauge to measure the size of the crab because you are not allowed to take undersized crab. The Canadian and the American gauges are different. Use the appropriate one.

We usually cook the crabs in salt water in a big pot. We use butter and lemon. Yum...

Shrimp pots:

If you don't have a puller on your dinghy forget shrimp. 400 feet is a lot of line to pull over the side. A puller makes all the difference. Also it's darn handy to have a small fish finder on the dinghy.

Diesel engine maintenance:

- Change your Jabsco impeller before you go and make sure you have 2 spares.

- Make sure you have two spare belts for your alternator and salt-water pump.

- Replace your large fuel filter and carry 4 spares.

- Fuel: If your fuel has been sitting in the tanks for more than a year, either pump it between the tanks with a filter or have it polished. This is VERY important. Most boats get into trouble when they hit bumpy water and the gunk in the tank comes unstuck and clogs the fuel filter. Motor stops. 2 motors 2 stops. Some clever boat men have dual filters with a switch. Yep they are the smart ones. Not so much of a problem if you have a polisher.

(When the boat bounces around a lot the gunk on the bottom mixes up and clogs the filters and your engine stops.)

Some silly things to remember:

- One:

Buy the Canadian Current Tables volumes 5 and 6. Remember Canadians love to watch Americans misread the tables. Canadian tables are not corrected for Daylight Savings Time; you must add one hour. The Secondary Tide Tables are a bit strange, so have a Canadian explain how to use them. . But if you can't find a Canadian or just don't want to ask try this...

To use a secondary tide table, you're given a page number for the primary tide and a time correction to go with it.

 For instance, add 24 minutes for flood and 22 minutes for ebb based on the Port Atkinson tide station referred to by page number in the Tide Table.

- Two:

Buy the American book "Ports and Passes". This book has a nice big column of slack tides at the major narrows and is corrected for Daylight Savings Time.

- Three:

Desolation Sound at Refuge Cove marks the change in the direction of currents. Flood currents go south, ebb currents go north. So if you're going north you have to think opposite from what you are used to. If you have been sailing south of Desolation Sound you have to reverse your thinking and catch ebb tide and ride it north.

- Four:

Arrive at narrows one hour before slack. Arrive early because sometimes tugs are pulling log booms through the channels and you have to wait. If you are going with the tide, you can usually leave twenty minutes before slack. If you are going against the current you usually have to wait for boats transiting from the other direction.

When approaching the narrows, one uses the radio to declare for example, "Securite, Securite, Motor Vessel Star Rover transiting north through Dodd Narrows."

- Five:

Cruising is all about currents. Take a ride on the Reading! Nobeltec is the only software I know that has wonderful current arrows that increase in size as the current gets stronger. You can advance the time and date on the computer and study the current changes. We will go into detail on riding the currents in different chapters. Currents are your allies if you're going in the right direction. Currents can also be scary and unpleasant.

stuff you might have forgotten

- Wrenches for drip shaft

- Fuel filter wrenches

- Topping off distilled water in the batteries

- Mosquito nets for all hatches

- Plastic screen for main hatch

- 12 volt fans for cool sleeping

- Light day packs for hiking (first aid kit-Deet-knife-fire starter-water bottle-compass)

- After bite spray for mosquito bites

- Mosquito spray pepper spray for bears

- Sun block

- Rain and sun hats

- Gaffer or duct tape

- Spare clamps for engine hoses

- Anchor for dinghy

- It's good to have some sort of spare prop.

Permits you want to and have to have

Glacier Bay

Visitors bringing their own boat into Glacier Bay from June 1 through August 31 must have a permit and reservations.

If you are considering a trip to Glacier Bay you should book a permit and reservation at the earliest possible time.

http://www.NPS.gov

Anan Wildlife Observatory

The web site says it all …. "From July 5 through August 25, an individual pass is required to visit the wildlife observatory. Visitation outside this time period does not require a reservation or pass. For reservation information, please go to the reservation page. During the peak-viewing season of July and August, Forest Service interpreters are on-site to provide current information on bear safety, trail conditions, and bear activity. For your safety, some special cautions and restrictions are necessary. Close encounters with bears using the Anan Trail are not infrequent from June 15 to September 15."

We'll say more below but Anan is a great place to visit and you shouldn't miss it. The bears are there, the salmon are there; Anan is fabulous.

http://www.fs.fed.us/r10/tongass/recreation/wildlife_viewing/ananobs ervatory.shtml

The six essentials of cruising to Alaska

- **Anchor and chain and winch must work**. Makes life much easier and if your motor stops suddenly you'll want to anchor as quickly as possible. If you're in a tight spot this can prevent a disaster.

- **Know where you are at all times**. Even if you're just using a GPS and a chart, mark your position every hour; keep your eye on all navigational buoys until you round the mark.

- **Know the currents**. Traverse the narrows at slack or one hour before with the current. Use the current to push you where you want to go. A two-knot current can mean the difference between 6 hours of travel and 8 hours of travel.

- **Your motor must run**. You will be using your motor at least 60 per cent of the time on your travel to Alaska. Know your fuel range. Get fuel before you need it. You're going to need your motor running to get where you want to go.

- Note: It is not a bad idea to attach a motor bracket onto your transom. You can attach your outboard and make at least 3 knots as long as you have gas. That way you can at least get out of the harbor and get your sails up.

- **You need a dinghy and or a kayak**. Don't buy a weird **dinghy**. There is a reason why 95 percent of boaters have a rubber dinghy. It is because they are incredibly stable. Having a dinghy is a safety issue. If the boat sinks you need something to get into. **Kayaks** are great when you need exercise. The plastic ones like the Loon weigh only 35 lbs. and you can throw them over the side. Another reason we like plastic kayaks is that we can run them right up on the beach. An **outboard** is handy as rowing a rubber dinghy in wind is not pleasant. Electric motors are becoming popular as carrying gas is a drag.

- **Don't fall in the water.** Remember if you fall into the water at 39 degrees you have 30 minutes at best before you become a log. Keep one hand for the boat always.

- **Keep watch at all times**! Cruise ships travel at 25 knots. That means they can come out of nowhere in 10 minutes! Fishing boats rarely have anyone steering. It sometimes seems that they simply don't bother to try to miss you. Maybe they think it's fun to try and scare you. Powerboats sometimes do not see sailboats. While you're freezing to death, they're down below taking showers and eating frozen dinners.

Clearing Customs into British Columbia

Note: you must make your first stop in Canada at a designated customs stop!

We usually clear customs at Poet's Cove (Bedwell Harbour) on Pender Island.

Remember only the captain can get off the boat until you clear customs.

You go to the customs dock and pick up the phone by the booth.

Here are the questions they usually ask and the information they normally want:

- Where are you?

- Where did you come from?

- Name of boat

- Make of boat

- Length of boat

- How long are you staying in Canada?

- Name of captain

- Cell phone number

- Home address

- Boat number or document number

- Passport number

- Passport expiration date

- How many passengers aboard? (All must have passports)

- Are there firearms on board? (No handguns permitted)

- Do you have bear spray on board? (Not permitted)

- Whiskey and spirits? (Only 24 beers or one liter of spirits or wine per person)

- Are you carrying less than 10,000 Canadian dollars?

- Are you carrying anything for sale in Canada?

- There are restrictions on fresh apples, stone fruit and potatoes

In British Columbia I have found the Customs Agents to be courteous and respectful, however...

You really do not want to get on their bad boy list or you will be searched every time you go to Canada. So be truthful.

If you have two bottles of Scotch just say so.

One last note:

If you have DUIs or felony charges do not go to Canada. If any of your passengers have DUIs they will not be permitted into Canada.

If you want to carry a shotgun it's easier to ship it by air to a port in Alaska and have it stored until you get there.

Section Two: The direct (and fast) way North

These are my favorite places to stop from Nanaimo to Bella Bella.

- Nanaimo

- Campbell River

- Port Harvey

- Malcolm Island

- Port Hardy – if the wind is blowing fresh from north

- Fury Cove

- Pruth – a pretty beach but a bit out of the way

- Codville Lagoon – a cool place

- Bella Bella and Shearwater Marina

The fastest way north is to leave Nanaimo and go up Seymour Narrows to Race Passage. Use the current flowing north on the ebb to shoot up to Johnston Straits across Point Conception to Fury Cove and then up to Bella Bella and Shearwater Marina. The passage takes about six days.

Nanaimo:

The main concern leaving Nanaimo is to make sure Whiskey Gulf (WG) is not active. WG is an area just outside of Nanaimo that is a gunnery range for the Canadian navy. The Canadians take transgression as seriously bad behavior. One listens to the weather channel 1 to 5 to make sure it is clear to transit Whiskey Gulf.

 The other concern to keep in mind is the gulf can get nasty with the wind above 20 knots. It is best to leave at 5 in the morning when the forecast is for light winds. We have gotten the S***t kicked out of us and had a hell of a time reefing the main with the boat being stood up on end. Best prepare by putting in a reef in the main and throwing all the loose stuff into the sink. Batten down. You are probably going to get it.

Thrifty supermarket	To the left of the marina past the ferry to the Dinghy Dock Pub.
Liquor	Next to Thrifty
Chandlery	Largest chandlery on Vancouver Island. Very helpful
Restaurants	Acme, Modern, hot dog stand across from library.
Coffee/Wi-Fi	In town across from Modern Cafe

http://www.harbourchandler.ca

http://www.acmefoodco.ca

http://www.thriftyfoods.com/EN/main/locations/nanaimo-port-place.html

http://moderncafe.foodpages.ca/

From Nanaimo to Campbell River is a long day.

Campbell River:

The dock rates are buck a foot. Some of the slips are quite small and hard to get into. You do not have to take the first one offered.

Campbell River Discovery Harbour Marina

Supermarket	Canadian Superstore (huge). My advice is don't buy any yellow generic products because they suck.
Shopping mall	Yes
Showers	At the dock Discovery Harbour Marina
Toilets	Behind the office for the marina.
Pump out	At the dock of the Discovery Harbour Marina
Fuel (diesel)	North side of Discovery Harbour (Esso)
Liquor store	Up the ramp by the office
Restaurants	Good pub at top of the ramp
Coffee with Wi-Fi	Starbucks one block right at stairs.
Chandlers	In town – West Marine
Water	Good
Getting around	You walk

Heading out you go north from Campbell River through Seymour

Narrows.

Seymour Narrows:

Tidal streams can attain 16 knots. Remember the ebb goes north and the flood goes south. Seymour Narrows can be tough.

The strategy is to pick a day you can leave early and get to the narrows 1 hour before slack, preferably before 10:00 AM. Stay away from Ripple Rock, check that the water is relatively smooth, and head north. (When transiting south, use Duncan and Menzies Bays to wait for the current to ease to 3 knots.)

Chatham Point:

The junction of Discovery Pass and Johnston Straits and can have steep choppy seas during a strong ebb.

Race Passage:

Race Passage is preferred over Current Passage. Race can have 6 or more knots on ebb and 5 or more on flood. If the wind is opposing the current the ride can get bumpy but we still prefer to stay on the Race side.

On the north side of Race Passage you can put in at Kelsy Bay. Kelsy Bay is crowded with boats and it has strong currents. Generally you just tie up next to anyone you can and then check in with the Warfinger. Rate was $0.50 Canadian a foot.

Johnstone Straits:

The radio almost always says *gale warnings*.

If you're going north and the wind is from the south, it's probably good to go. What you don't want to do is sail into a strong northerly blowing 30 knots. Northerlies are no fun, wait it out.

Port Neville:

Port Neville is the first port in Johnstone Strait after Kelsy Bay. It is not a great anchorage but it is protected from the northerlies. Get onto the dock if you can.

Port Harvey:

If you have to get out of Johnstone Strait, Port Harvey, with its good anchorage, is a much better choice than Port Neville. Harvey has a small store and fuel.

If you can make it all the way up Johnstone Straits to Port McNeill you're looking good.

Port McNeill:

Anchoring outside of the bay is permitted. Stay clear of lumbering operations.

Restaurants	Up from the dock
Market	Thrifty – 2 blocks up from dock
Showers	In the parking lot above the government dock
Toilets	Public toilets in the park
Pump out	Government dock
Fuel (diesel)	Yes great prices. Best place to fill up going north. Ice at fuel dock.
Liquor	Yes just before supermarket
Coffee with Wi-Fi	Coffee shop up from dock about two blocks

Chandlers	Good auto parts/Chandlery across from helicopters.
Water	Good
Getting around	Bike and car rental

Note: I prefer to leave Port McNeill and continue on to Sointula on Malcolm Island as soon as I get fuel. It's about an hour away.

Sointula, Malcolm Island:

A small craft harbor at the north end of Malcolm Island on Rough Bay.

Supermarket Co-op	Great Co-op about two kilometers from harbor. Use one of the purple bikes if possible.
Bakery	Excellent - across from the Co-op
Showers	At dock
Toilets	At dock
Laundry	At dock
Liquor	Yes – at the Sointula Co-op Store
Book store	At museum – used books
Book exchange	In laundry at the dock
Entertainment	The Rub Pub – live music
Restaurants	Burger Barn at the dock and the

	Cafe in town – good food
Coffee with Wi-Fi	Café with Wi-Fi in town
Chandlers	Some limited supplies at Co-op
Water	Tastes funny
Hikes	Great walks and good hikes from the town. Check out Beautiful Bay (You'll have to take a cab but it's worth it.)

Malcolm Island is called the Island of Harmony and it's a delightful place to stay. The harbor is excellent and the Warfingers are pleasant. The Burger Barn at the head of the dock is great for hamburgers and fish and chips. Take the hike to Beautiful Bay. It's wonderful.

Port Hardy:

From Malcolm Island and Sointula it's about a 5-hour beat northward to Port Hardy – the northernmost port on Vancouver Island. Hardy is a good port to get provisions, fuel and water if you haven't done so already at Port McNeil or Malcolm. You can stay at God's Pocket a bit north of Hardy for a spot more scenic for your liftoff from Vancouver Island to the real wilderness of Northern British Columbia.

Getting to Port Hardy can be a hard sail if there's a strong northerly blowing. Once I had a friend fly in to Port McNeil as his jump-off point. We left late to get to Port Hardy and bucked a northerly all the way up. By the time we got to Hardy he was ready to go home. A little coaxing got him to stay and we ended up having a great trip to Bella Bella, but it was only after a good night's rest at Port Hardy.

When you get past Vancouver Island, you really only have provisions and fuel at Bella Bella before you head off to Prince Rupert about a week away. Prince Rupert is the Canadian city furthest north on the Inside Passage.

Port Hardy to Fury Cove:

Advice for crossing Cape Caution from an old fisherman:

"Don't do what the Yachties do which is to sail out at 10 AM on a bright sunny day. It looks good but you'll take it in the shorts when Queen Charlotte blows up in the afternoon. Do just the opposite, what the fishermen do, go out early on drizzle and calm."

When we head out we go by Pine Island, and Storm Island, to Egg Island. There is a set that pushes you easterly towards Egg Island so you need to compensate. Once clear of Pine Island, we head up for Fury Cove at the beginning of Fitz Hugh Sound on the right just past Rivers Inlet.

Note to fishermen:

Rivers Inlet is where we rig the electric down rigger, nets and fishing poles as there is fine fishing from here to Alaska.

Fury Cove:

We generally put into Fury Cove (Schooner Retreat on Chart 3934).

Entering the first time is a bit daunting. First off identify Rouse Reef. South of Rouse Reef is Rouse Point. It is best to avoid Breaker Pass and enter to the south of Cleave Island. Once inside hook around to the left and then head around the back of Fury Island through a narrow pass into Fury Cove. There are generally 4 or 5 boats at anchor. The cove is well protected, has a lovely beach, and gives a great view out into Fitz Hugh Sound. We fish around the end of Penrose Island and also up Rivers Inlet to Dawson Bay. Once back in Fritz we've ducked into Fish Egg Inlet for a few nice kings and then we meander up to Pruth Bay.

Pruth Bay:

Pruth Bay is an excellent stop, and it's worth going all the way down the channel to anchor. Hike out to the outer exposed beach about a mile east from the harbor. Looks like some Bali Hi place out in the Pacific with its white sand.

Codville Lagoon:

From **Pruth** we usually hop up to Codville Lagoon. The entrance is small (stay south) and hard to see, but well worth the stop. We proceed around Codville Island anchor at the north end of the lagoon. There are usually lots of sea lions on the rocks just south of Codville Island and we put our crab traps out just inside the entrance before we head up to anchor.

Bella Bella and Shearwater Marina:

From **Codville** we head up through Lama Passage to Bella Bella. We usually get water, diesel, and food supplies at the Native store. Once we're fixed up, we proceed to Shearwater Marina.

Shearwater Marina has a good dock but it's often crowded. The restaurant and bar are good and there's a moderate sized store, some boating supplies, shower, and laundry.

A great detour on the main route: Fjordland

This detour is lovely and adds about 2 days to the trip. It is well worth it just to experience Kynoch Waterfall.

Exit **Bella Bella** out Seaforth Channel to Ivory Island. You can go up the narrow Reid Passage. We were lucky to be travelling with fellows familiar with the area. You transit around Ivory Island, clear Mouse Rocks, and go up Mathieson Channel to Percival Narrows.

From Percival Narrows go past Oscar Passage to Rescue Bay – a large, good holding, and well sheltered bay. (Chart 3724). Rescue Bay is at the head of Jackson Passage. The next day, you can motor up Mathieson Channel past Griffin to **Kynoch Inlet**. At the head of Kynoch is a spectacular waterfall.

Proceed down Kynoch Inlet to its end – **Culpepper Lagoon**. The anchorage is small and you'll be on a shelf just off the beach. Make sure your anchor is set as the wind comes howling down the fjord. (See the story *"The Parrot's Beak"* in the last section of the book.) It is possible to enter the Lagoon at high slack with anchorage just inside. The Lagoon is huge so we opted to explore Culpepper by dinghy.

From Culpepper you go back north. Exit out **Kynoch** to **Mathieson** and then north from the narrows to **Sheep Passage** (Chart 3738) and to **Carter Bay** (a good place to stop on the way back out).

It is then a full day to **Keekane** opposite **Butedale**. You need to go around the sand spit as you enter Keekane and proceed up the bay to the end opposite the waterfall. There is good mud at the mouth of the river. From Keekane, we go to **Bishop Bay Hot Springs**. Bishop is crowded and has a small dock so try and get there early. You may have to anchor to the right of the dock until someone leaves.

From Bishop Bay Hot Springs you go back down Ursula to McKay Reach and up to **Hartley Bay** for fuel and water. From Hartley, we go back down to Wright sound through the slot past Coghlatt Point, and then hook to the north up Greenville Channel stopping in **Lowe** or **Klewnuggitt Inlet** for the night. Lowe has a lovely stream running through it and a lovely lake. We anchor over to the right of the stream by the shore beach. Be careful as it gets shallow quickly. The mud has good holding. **Baker Inlet** is another alternative stopping place. Next morning proceed up through Watts Narrows, or up to **Kumealon Inlet**, then traverse up **Grenville**, past **Gunboat**, on through Arthur to **Prince Rupert.**

Rupert to Ketchikan:

Going north to Ketchikan from Prince Rupert, we travel via **Venn Channel** (it is best to go at slack or with the See Chart 3955 and 3557..

Once clear of Venn we head north towards Dundas on the Canadian side and Foggy Bay on the American side.

Dundas or *Foggy Bay:*

Some notes on crossing back into America:

The first certified Customs port in America after leaving Prince Rupert is Ketchikan. Officially that is where you have to stop before anchoring in American waters.

It's a long haul to Ketchikan and most of us try to sleep over in Foggy Bay. Foggy Bay is tricky to get into the first time. You need to go around a reef that is just below the waterline. It helps to go behind someone who leads you. Once inside, it is a fine harbor.

However, that being said, you need to call customs in Ketchikan and get permission to anchor in Foggy Bay because Foggy Bay is in the USA. Technically if you put your anchor down in the mud you are landed and you need to clear Customs before you are landed. (It's stupid, I know.)

If you don't receive permission from the Customs Agents for Foggy Bay you need to stop in Brundige Inlet on Dundas Island. Brundige Inlet is a narrow 4-kilometer channel on the north side of Dundas. For the longest time I resisted going in as I thought there were navigation issues. Actually it's pretty straightforward. You go in; you go up ¾ of the channel and anchor in mud at about 30 feet. Aside from getting bit by every "no-see-em" in the world, you'll have a pleasant night's sleep. (If you remembered to bring the screens.) Since Dundas is Canada, there are no problems.

Next day be sure to leave early as it's still a full day to Ketchikan. Make sure you listen to the weather as you'll be crossing open water for 30 miles or so. It's usually good sailing out of Dundas as with any luck you're on a reach.

Ketchikan:

Once in Ketchikan you need to clear customs. We stop at the lower harbor (Thomas Basin) south of the cruise ships and walk to the pink customs house.

After clearing customs go out around the cruise ships to **Bar Harbor** about a mile north of town. The main reasons for staying in Bar Harbor are:

- No cruise ships

- No people from the cruise ships

- Convenient Safeway Supermarket a short ways south

- There is Liquor next to Safeway

- Restaurants and bars

- Showers

- Laundry

For fuel you need to stop at the Texaco dock north of Bar Harbour.Note for you hikers: There is a wonderful trail just outside of town up Mt Dude. It is a fabulous hike and gives you a spectacular view of Ketchikan from the mountaintop. You need to rent a car.

http://www.seatrails.org/com_ketchikan/trl-dude.htm

Mt Dude – Ketchikan

Ketchikan

Ketchikan to Petersburg

- Ketchikan

- Meyers Chuck – if it's blowing from the north

- Thorne Bay

- Anan

- Wrangell

- St John Harbor – across from Wrangell Narrows

- Wrangell Narrows – also known as Christmas Tree Lane
  - Enter one hour before the last of the flood
  - Chart 17375

- Petersburg

It's a bit of a challenge to get out of Ketchikan. The wind is usually blowing from the north at about 25 knots and the sea is bumpy so you might find yourself putting into **Meyers Chuck** for a rest. Chuck is a nice little harbor surrounded by reefs at the entrance. It has a small dock and a gift shop. It's a pleasant place to spend the night and it's fun to hike around the settlement.

Going north from Meyers Chuck, we've stopped in **Thorne Bay**. It's a ways in and a bit shallow in places but once you get inside it's a good anchorage. We've also stopped at Ratz Harbor but didn't like it nearly as well and it's exposed to the swell. The rocky bottom made it difficult to anchor.

Leaving Throne Bay, we proceed up Clarence to Stikene Strait and then through Chichagof Passage to Wrangell.

Wrangell:

We have come to appreciate **Wrangell**. The old harbor is preferred as it is close to town. Don't go to the inside bay! It is shallow. We get fuel on the way in, and then go across and tie up at the government dock.

There is a fine supermarket in town, but it's tucked away off the main street.

The Wrangell Museum is quite remarkable and well worth visiting. The other reason for stopping at Wrangell is to secure a permit for **Anan** if you don't have one yet.

ANAN

http://www.fs.fed.us/r10/tongass/recreation/wildlife_viewing/ananobs ervatory.shtml

More from the web site: "The bounty of the summer salmon run supports the magnificent wildlife viewing at Anan. Anan Creek has the largest run of pink salmon in Southeast Alaska. It is estimated that 300,000 fish make their way up the creek to spawn and die. Shortly after hatching, pink salmon fry head to the ocean. Pinks spend about 2 years in the ocean before returning to their natal creek to spawn."

It's about three hours by boat down to the observatory from Wrangell. At Anan, you anchor and take your dinghy in to shore. Once on shore you talk to the ranger before going up the hour walk to the observation platform.

The numbers of salmon are unbelievable. You can walk across their backs to cross a stream! Many brown and black bears come to feast on the salmon as do lots of eagles. From the secure viewing platform and house you can see them all – almost, but not quite, near enough to touch. ***Don't miss Anan!***

The Bears at Anan

Wrangell to Petersburg:

Going north from Wrangell we stop at **Saint John Harbor** across from Wrangell Narrows.

We like St. John because it's quiet and out of the way from the large volume of traffic going up **Christmas Tree Lane**. Christmas Tree has 66 navigational aids, which gives you some idea of how complex and interesting the channel is. If it's foggy do not go. The best time to transit from either end is one hour before the end of the flood tide.

Once through the Wrangell Narrows (Christmas Tree Lane), you arrive in **Petersburg**. We usually stay right at **North Harbor** with the not so great smelling cannery. You need to call the harbormaster to get a slip assignment. If you can, book a ride to LeConte Glacier, or go halibut fishing. Both trips are fantastic.

LeConte Glacier

http://en.wikipedia.org/wiki/LeConte_Glacier

Petersburg to Glacier Bay – the direct route

- Petersburg

- Baranof Warm Springs

- Tenakee Springs

- Bartlett Cove - Glacier Bay

Leave Petersburg early in the morning, and head north up Frederick Sound to Point Gardner into Chatham Straits then up a short way to Baranof Island. There are a profusion of wild things, particularly humpback whales all over the place. The confluence of Frederick and Chatham can be quite bumpy. It behooves the prudent mariner to not beat north in Chatham when the wind is up. You can duck into Portage Bay if the wind is bad. Usually mornings are calmer. **Baranof** has wonderful hot springs. The dock is usually crowded. We have anchored in the small bay to the left after you enter. Be sure and hike up to the upper baths as they are HOT and pristine.

http://www.sederquist.com/alaska2004/baranof.html

http://www.tenakeespringsak.com

Baranof Warm Springs Hot Tub

Baranof Warm Springs

Assuming you can make it out from Baranof into Chatham before the wind freshens; you can beat up Chatham, and enter **Tenakee Springs Bay**. The town has a lovely boardwalk and the harbor is huge.

Tenakee General Store

The springs at Tenakee may not be on par with Baranof but there's great hiking along the boardwalk and the harbor offers protection from the north wind.

From Tenakee you've got a long beat up to Chatham Strait, around Point Adolphus, into Icy Straits and then **Bartlett Cove**.

Welcome to Tenakee

GLACIER BAY

Bartlett Cove

Glacier Bay National Park and Preserve

"... a World Heritage Site in the United States — is a 3.3 million acre treasure of natural wonders and wildlife near Juneau, Alaska. Magnificent glaciers... towering snow-capped mountains... abundant birds and wildlife... and mile after mile of pristine coastline. Whether you are here for a day or a week, you'll find endless opportunities for discovery and adventure here. Glacier Bay Lodge, nestled under the spruce trees that line Bartlett Cove, offers the only hotel accommodations within the park."

http://www.visitglacierbay.com

Bartlett Cove, just outside the Glacier Bay Lodge, is the favored anchorage while awaiting the mandatory check-in lecture. The Lodge has a fine restaurant and gift shop. Travelers from all over the world come to Glacier Bay and stay at the Lodge. It's a friendly place and you'll get to meet and chat with a lot of interesting people: kayakers, photographers, naturalists, etc. etc.

Your permit gives you 7 cruising days in a spectacular area limited to 12 boats, excluding tour boats and there aren't that many of them either. There are no crowds, lots of wildlife, fishing and kayaking. The National Park does a fabulous job of limiting access and ensuring a wonderful adventure in one of the most spectacular places to visit in Alaska.

We went for broke and motored all the way up to the top of Glacier Bay to anchor at **Reid Glacier** just inside the jetty protecting the harbor. We were alone for two days and then another two boats came in and anchored near Reid Glacier. This was our base camp for Glacier exploration and a fabulous place for hikes and adventure. We chose to explore all the glaciers at the end of the park during the day. We got up close to **Reid** and **Lamplugh Glaciers.** Johns Hopkins Inlet was iced up so we couldn't get to **Johns Hopkins Glacier** – a glacier that is one the very few that is not retreating and actually growing.

We turned and went up **Tarr Inlet** to **Margerie Glacier**; we ended up at **Grand Pacific Glacier**. While up the Tarr Inlet we got nudged out of position by a huge tour boat.

It is amazing how quiet they are and they can sneak up on you; that night we returned to Reid as there are not a lot of safe anchorages up at the end of Glacier Bay.

On our way back down and out we stopped overnight at Geikie Inlet and anchored in Shag Cove. We didn't want to ever leave.

Section Three: Taking your time going north

In this section we're taking it easy and not going off in a big rush to get to Alaska. Indeed, some of the best cruising sights are along the way.

Instead of going left to Campbell River from Nanaimo, we head out across the Strait of Georgia over to Entrance Island on the BC mainland side. We go up Malaspina Strait by Texada Island to **Pender**.

From Pender we go to **Princess Louisa**, then to **Desolation Sound** and up through the three rapids (Yaculta, Gillard and Dent) to Shoal Bay.

Leaving Shoal Bay we go past two more rapids (Green Rapids and Whirlpool Rapids) to Johnstone Straits. At Port Harvey, we turn to starboard and go into the **Broughton Islands**.

After cruising in the Broughtons we go to Port Hardy, and then up to Bella Bella.

Places along the way:

- Nanaimo
- Pender
- Egmont
- Princess Louisa
- Lund
- Desolation Sound

  o Squirrel Cove

  o The Gorge

  o Prideaux haven

- Roscoe Bay

- Refuge Cove

The three scary rapids: Yaculta, Gillard and Dent-**Transit at Slack!**

- Shoal Bay
- Forward Harbor
- Port Harvey
- The Broughton Islands:

  - Kwatsi

  - Laura

  - Shaw

  - Echo

  - Sullivan

- Malcolm Island and Sointula
- Fury Cove

  - Fish Egg Inlet

  - Pruth

  - Codville Lagoon

- Bella Bella -Shearwater Marina

Star Rover

Leaving Nanaimo:

More information on Nanaimo is in the section above, *A Fast Way North.*

Before you leave Nanaimo make the time to go to **Newcastle Island** and do the hikes. You can go completely around the island and in and around the middle. Bring a picnic lunch.

When you're getting ready to leave Nanaimo check the weather channel 1-5 for calm winds or 5 to 10 SW and make sure Whisky Gulf is not active.

There is no shame is motoring across the Strait of Georgia in calm weather. If the straits are having a bad day you may be in for a rough ride. Batten down everything inside. Throw the cups in the sink. Get everything off the counters and the stove.

There's plenty of good sailing once you get close to the Welcome Islands. If the wind builds from the north, you can go into Secret Cove and anchor, otherwise continue up Malaspina Straits along Texada Island to Pender Harbor.

Pender:

Once inside Pender, we like Fisherman's Dock. The folks at Fisherman's are pleasant and the marina has showers, a laundry, a medium sized store, fuel, and a good restaurant within walking distance. Prices at the marina are a dollar a foot. http://www.fishermansresortmarina.com

If you want groceries from the local supermarket you must get in your dinghy or kayak and row across the bay to the Government Wharf. There you'll find another marina, and a short walk takes you to a park, a coffee shop, art gallery, bakery and supermarket.

The next morning you can exit Pender and take the first channel, Agamemnon, to Egmont which is about 4 hours motoring.

Egmont:

Stop at the dock with fuel and the sign "Backeddy Pub". Back Eddy Resort & Marina - Egmont, BC, on the Sunshine Coast...

http://www.bigpacific.com/pender/egmont.html

http://www.env.gov.bc.ca/bcparks/explore/parkpgs/skook_narrows/

http://www.backeddy.ca

We had some of the best fish and chips of the entire trip at the pub.

If you can spare the time, take a hike down to **Skookumchuck Narrows.** Established in 1957 Skookumchuck Narrows Provincial Park has trails and viewing areas that show off the power of the incredibly turbulent tidal rapids. On a 3-meter tide, 200 billion gallons of water flow through the narrows connecting Sechelt and Jervis Inlet. Sometimes there's a better than 6 foot difference in water levels between one side of the rapids and the other. The current can move at over 18 mph. It is spectacularly impressive.

Once you leave Egmont, head towards Jervis inlet. Figure you need about 6 hours at 7 knots to motor up the Inlet and Queens Reach. There's really nowhere to stop on the way; it's helpful to sail up with another boat.

To get to the Princess you go through Malibu Rapids and ideally you want high tide slack. Slack at Malibu Rapids is calculated from Port Atkinson plus 30 minutes. Remember to add one hour if you are using the Canadian Tide Tables. Thus Port Atchenson is high at 7:00 AM then add one hour for 8:00 AM then add 30 minutes for slack.

Malibu Rapids is very narrow at low tide. It's kind of an "S" shaped passage. You'll pass a large lodge with a totem pole on your way in. Many people say *"Securite, Securite, sailing vessel *** transiting north."* When you're free of the rapids, you can sail up to the end of the fjord.

There's a government dock where you can tie up for 20 dollars a night. If it's crowded you can anchor to the right of the dock. If you go around the point you'll see some red circles on the rock. These are metal pins you can tie to.

If you decide to tie to the metal pins what we do is start in the deep water, let out a lot of chain and back in slowly. Then we take the kayak with our yellow floating line and tie the line to the metal pins. A spectacular anchorage is right below the small waterfall. We tie a "V" to two trees or the pins if you can find them.

Princess Louisa is truly one of the wonders of the earth. Don't miss it. It is a hassle to get there but it is one of the highlights of the trip to Alaska.

There are no facilities in the park other than an outhouse and camp area.

Things to do include the short hike up to the Chatterbox Falls, which is wonderful, and for a great adventure, get into the kayak and paddle up to the bottom of the falls. Watch for the birds – there are birds galore here.

If you want a fun crazy steep hike go to Chatterbox Falls and take the trail to the right leading up to the top of the canyon. It's gnarly and you're climbing up the wet and slippery tree roots but at the top, hidden from below, you look straight down the fjord to the Rapids. Awesome! There's floatplane service to Princess Louisa so you can also have crew or family fly in. However, radio and phone reception are zero, so you have to plan ahead of time. There's more about Princess Louisa in the story at the end of the book.

Chatterbox Falls at Princess Louisa Inlet

Dock at Princess Louisa

Rainforest at Princess Lousa

Louisa to Lund and the Copeland Islands Marine Park

Once you leave Princess Louisa, don't turn down Agamemnon Channel, go more or less straight out until you hit Malaspina Strait. You turn north and sail up past Grief Point to Lund and the Copeland Islands. If you have no time constraints for the next leg of the adventure, you can take your time and sail. Lund has a book exchange, a store, and a good bakery. The Copeland Islands are lovely. If you are careful, you can slip into one of the small nooks and anchor overnight.

The Desolation Sound

George Vancouver got a whole lot right when he explored the west coast of North America and the Inside Passage during his 1791-1795 trip – an amazing and incredible amount of stuff right. But he didn't get Desolation Sound right. At least not the name. Desolation Sound is spectacular.

The George:

After passing through a narrow entrance you'll enter a large bay surrounded by mountains on all sides. We anchor at the end of the bay by the lodge. The lodge has been refurbished and the setting is delightful. There is a fine restaurant (you might want to make reservations) and a good coffee shop called Trudy's behind the campground. The George has an excellent and well-stocked store just up from the marina. There are showers and a laundry with newer machines. Last trip we stayed two days and had a wonderful time.

Refuge Cove:

Is one of our tried and true friendly stops. Moorage is $0.60 a foot. There's fuel, propane, a small store, and a café. There's no hiking but good kayaking.

Squirrel Cove:

Squirrel Cove is right across the bay from Refuge. Enter only on the left channel. The dock is a short trip in the dinghy from the anchorage. Squirrel Cove has a good store with a nice walk-in freezer and there's a good restaurant too. You can deposit bags of garbage for a small fee.

Prideaux Haven:

Prideaux Haven is spectacular; but usually crowded. You can go around to Melanie or Laura Cove for more privacy.

Roscoe Bay Marine Park:

You must enter at high tide. The entrance is extremely shallow. You can stand in the middle at low tide. Once inside, the harbor is large and comfortable. Pretty much everywhere in the harbor is good anchorage.

Water is available from a hose connected to the waterfall near the entrance on the right as you enter. Once anchored, you can get in your dinghy and go to the beach opposite the entrance. You can walk up to Black Lake and enjoy wonderful swimming. The turnoff to the swimming spot is about ½ kilometer up the trail to the left. It helps to go with someone the first time. For extra fun, you can haul your kayak up onto Black Lake, have a wonderful paddle and with luck hear the cry of the Loons.

Once we have thoroughly enjoyed our stay at Roscoe, we usually go back to Refuge or Squirrel Cove. We then plan the next leg of our trip for the transit to Yaculta Rapids, which are about four hours north of Refuge.

Getting to Shoal Bay – the Three Rapids: Yaculta, Gillard and Dent

You'll hear a lot about the terrors of the Dent Rapids with the Devils Hole playing a prominent part in the horror.

For the prudent yachtsman it's really not difficult. Here are a few suggestions:

You should plan on motoring four hours up from Refuge Cove up Calm Channel to Yaculta. Ideally you want the current with you. Remember the ebb tide flows north.

All three rapids are only a short distance apart. You want to take Yaculta about 30 minutes early and then Gillard at 10 minutes dead slack followed by Dent 20 minutes later. You do want to avoid the Devils Hole which is to right and north of Gillard. You can then continue up to Shoal Bay.

Shoal Bay is a lovely government dock. The cost is 50 cents Canadian a foot. We definitely recommend going up to the pub and having a few beers at happy hour. The folks are fine conversationalists. Last trip we watched a lovely video of Janis Joplin. What fun. There's Wi-Fi at the lodge after 4:00 pm.

Shoal Bay to Forward Harbor

One of the reasons for stopping overnight at Shoal Bay is to time the next transit of Green and Whirlpool Rapids. Plan on transiting Green Rapids 30 minutes before slack and Whirlpool no later than 30 minutes past slack. We went through 1 hour after slack on the ebb and it was a bit scary, but not too bad. Once you are through Whirlpool you can turn into Forward Harbour and anchor on a sand shelf to the left as you enter.

Forward Harbor to Port Harvey

If you're heading down Sunderland Channel to Johnstone Strait, leave early in the morning. The wind usually comes up in the afternoon and if you can get down to Harvey before the wind comes up you'll have a pleasant voyage. Port Harvey has three good harbors, Open Cove being the first just around Harvey point but you can stay at any one of them. Relax and take a minute to plan for the Broughtons.

The Broughton Islands

It's good to have paper charts in the Broughton Islands! The Islands are complicated, they have a lot of channels and it's nice to see it all laid out. The Charts to bring are 3515 and 3547.

The morning after leaving Port Harvey, you can continue up to Chatham Narrows. Line up the range markers and stay to the center of the channel; it's deep enough. Don't be surprised if the current runs contrary to expectations in Chatham as Knight Inlet and Havannah Channel duke it out for current supremacy.

After you clear Chatham Narrows and Minstrel Island, you go across Knight Inlet and into Tribune Channel. Everything will get nice and calm and you can motor or sail up to Kwatsi Bay.

Kwatsi Bay:

Oh My God Bay in Kwatsi is spectacular and Max is always a pleasant host. Stay awhile.

Many times you can hook up with other boats sailing north. The idea in the Broughtons is to stay at least a week and talk to the other boaters and wander around in circles until one loses all sense of purpose.

Be advised there's not much in way of food or supplies in the Broughtons. Fuel is at Port Harvey, Echo Bay, and Sullivan Bay.

Provisions are pricy so best to have most of what you'll need with you. Many places have Wi-Fi but cell reception is poor.

Shaw Bay:

Shaw Bay is just around the corner from Kwatsi. Stay for pancake breakfast. After Shaw, there are dozens of small harbors like **Laura Bay** to duck into and stay awhile. The tradition at Kwatsi and other stops is to have a potluck at around 5:30. Chips and dips are the standard, but we've baked fresh bread and cookies to good effect and applause.

i

Kwatsi Potluck

Echo Bay:

Echo is a friendly, but crowded, stop with the bonus of movie night at the theater. You'll find fuel, beer, and groceries – home of the pig roast.

Green Bay:

Green Bay seems to be no longer functioning as a marina, but you can still stop there.

Another little cove to anchor is **Turnbull Cove** up Grappel Sound.

Sullivan Harbor:

Sullivan has a decent restaurant, showers, fuel and a medium sized store. It's a bit on the pricy side. Have lunch and try and jump across to **Drury Inlet**; it's a good place to get lost. Anchorage is behind the Muirhead islands on the north side and at Jennis Bay behind Hooper Island, about half way down. You must transit Stuart Narrows near slack!

Once you've run out of beer, groceries, and fuel it's time to head out of the Broughtons.

Napier Bay is a good anchorage before heading out into Queen Charlotte Strait to Port Hardy. Just like Johnstone Straits, head out in the early morning to avoid the northerly.

Going north from Port Hardy to Bella Bella is described earlier.

Section Four: The road less traveled to Prince Rupert

CHART 3744 is the big chart of the area north from Bella Bella.

The path we propose now is the wilder path up to Rupert from Bella Bella. If you look at the chart you'll see that Princess Royal Channel and Grenville Channels are VERY narrow. They're also the usual routes to Rupert as evidenced by all the traffic – a lot of it – including cruise ships and tugs.

The path we're suggesting is unusual, it's less traveled, not vey inhabited, and more beautiful than the standard route. It's still the Inside Passage, just a less known and used part of the Inside Passage.

- Bella Bella and Shearwater Marina
- Rescue Bay and Jackson Passage
- Klemtu around Swindle
- Meyers Passage
- Helmcken
- Mink Trap
- Anger Island
- Spider Island
- Prince Rupert

With this route there's just one bumpy bit of water across Caamano Sound; fog can be a problem. Travelers with good radar and lots of experience don't think twice and head out in the dense fog. However as the area is remote, we strongly recommend transiting with other boaters.

We go from Bella Bella to **Rescue Bay**, which is quite calm and secure with good fishing. At slack tide one heads into the very narrow Jackson Passage and goes across Finlayson and up the south of Cone Island to **Klemtu**.

Klemtu has good water, fuel, and an interesting Native American lodge. Leave Klemtu in the morning and transit around Split Head on Swindle Island and back south down to **Meyers Passage.**

Overnight at the harbor ¾ of the way down Meyers near **Cullum Point** and next morning set out up **Laredo Channel**.

Stops on the way are **Lelmken Inlet, Commando Inlet** or **Evinrude Inlet** but these may come up too soon. Continue up to **Estevan Sound,** up past **Otter Channel**. (Otter is a good place to cross back to Grenville Channel if you need to avoid the fog or get some fuel at Hartley Bay.)

If you stay in **Nepean Sound** you will continue up **Principe Channel** to **Anger Island**. **Patterson Inlet** is the preferred anchorage in this area with a shallow bottom and mud. (We have not tried it).

You then have the choice of which way to go around **McCauley Island**.

You can go to port up **Petrel Channel** and stop at **Newcombe Harbour** and **Captain Cove** , or you can go around the outside and continue up to **Spider Island**.

Spider is an excellent overnight stop with good fishing and one day passage up **Ogden Channel** to Prince Rupert.

The saying goes,

" If you want it stop raining in *Prince Rupert*, you have to leave."

Prince Rupert

We always have trouble finding a place to tie up in Rupert. We usually get thrown out of the first anchorage at the yacht club because we did not reserve a slip one month in advance. It is very bumpy on the outside as the fishermen think it's funny to go roaring past. We usually go down to the government dock about 1 mile south of town. It's always crowded. With luck you can raft onto someone. It is a good hike into town but you are rewarded with fine pubs, supermarkets, theaters, and coffee shops with Wi-Fi. If you brought your folding bike with the basket for groceries, you win!

http://www.visitprincerupert.com/

http://www.breakerspub.ca/

We usually end up getting hammered at Breakers Pub, and then wander into town to the supermarket, liquor store, and Wi-Fi coffee shop at Third Avenue Coffee.

After a week of rain, and doing the laundry you can hit the trail.

Off to Alaska

Glacier National Park

Glacier Bay Alaska

Mendenhall Glacier

Some interesting detours

Even when you're taking your time you sometimes can't do everything. Here are 3 "detours" on the slow way north that, if you can, you should take.

Detour # 1: Baranof Warm Springs to Sitka

It's all about fishing.

Going to Sitka from Baranof Warm Springs: figure two days up, four days in Sitka, two days travel back to Tenakee.

The route is up Peril Strait with a stop at the top of Sergius Narrows in the lovely Deep Bay.

The main attraction of **Sitka** is incredible fishing. Sportsmen come from all over the world to fish these waters. Go out on your own boat or travel with a guide. Either way you won't be disappointed.

If you're there with a fisherman and you're ready to let them go off on their own you'll find some lovely sites in Sitka. The Russian influence is clear and interesting. The bay is lovely and the library is good. There are good restaurants, bars, and groceries too. Just walking around is worth being there. Just pick up the Sitka info guides and do what they suggest.

Cruise boats do stop at Sitka so plan to get out of town (or be out of town) when 3 of them show up.

Detour #2: An alternate route to Glacier Bay:

Petersburg to Juneau to Glacier Bay

In the event you can't secure a permit to Glacier Bay there is an alternative. You can go around the starboard side of Admiralty Island.This alternative route lets you see some spectacular glaciers on the way up to Juneau. Once you hit Auke Bay to the north of Juneau, you can still book a passage to Glacier Bay on one of the commercial tours.

Begin at **Petersburg**:

From there you can visit the southernmost Glacier in Alaska – LeConte.

LeConte Glacier is spectacular and there are no restrictions. (Check out the picture up above.) You can take your boat up to the glacier but the entrance is tricky and there are few good anchorages. We recommend you take an aluminum tour boat even though it may seem expensive.

It's quite an experience to go with the tour guys because they use their boats to push their way up through the burgee bits right close to the glacier. They can fire along at 30 knots so the trip is about an hour down and an hour back from Petersburg, with two hours spent at the Glacier. A lot faster than you could make on your own.

Taku:

From Petersburg we go to Taku where you can tie up at the Government Wharf. There are good hikes and fine photo ops exploring the abandoned cannery.

Tracy Arm:

From *Taku* we go to *Tracy Arm* and up to the *North Sawyer Glacier*. There is an anchorage just inside the entrance to Tracy to the left but once inside Tracy the water turns VERY cold and there are many chunks of ice floating down the inlet and out to sea.

It is an all day trip up to the glacier and it's wonderful. We go up and down in one day and return to Taku where it is an easy tie up.

Tracy Arm

Adventurous souls can go down Tracy Arm and into **Fords Terror**. Further down the bay are **Endicott Arm** and **Dawes Glacier**. We haven't gone there but we hear it is wild!

Juneau:

After leaving Tracy Arm we head up to Juneau. Our opinion is to avoid town when the cruise ships are in port.

Juneau is an O.K. town and we like to hang out for a day or two. There is a cable car – the Mount Roberts Tramway – that offers spectacular views.

http://www.traveljuneau.com/

A must see trip is a visit to **Mendenhall Glacier** just outside of town. You can take the Glacier Express Blue Bus from town. Take your hiking stuff and spend a whole day. Great trip! If you are crazy you can even rent a car and take your dinghy or kayak and go right up to the Glacier. Oh yes!

http://www.fs.fed.us/r10/tongass/districts/mendenhall/

After doing the sights we head out to Auke, our much preferred harbor and about four hours north of Juneau.

Auke Bay Harbor:

The harbor brochure says it all: "This moorage facility is located 12 miles to the north of Juneau. The harbor is connected to town by road. The Don D. Statter Harbor facilities provide 6,000' of transient moorage for boats up to 200' in length. Moorage is on a first-come, first-served basis. Register at the Harbor Master's office (located at the head of the floats for transient moorage. The Length of stay is 10 days maximum moorage allowed or you could be cited for over-staying. Water, showers, and pump-out are available. Showers and carts are found at the Harbor Office. Office hours from May-Sept 30th are from 8 am - 4:30 pm 7 days a week. Saturday & Sunday closed 1 hour for lunch." Phone: 907-789-0819

You will find many fancy boats with paid crews awaiting their owners for the trip to Glacier Bay. With no permits, your option is to book a day tour on a jet boat to Glacier Bay. We stayed 5 days in the harbor, and enjoyed the inexpensive restaurants and friendly sailors.

Auke

Restaurants	Yes at head of dock
Market	Need to go to Juneau
Fuel	Yes but crowded go early in the AM
Water	good
Showers	dock
Hike	Take the bus to Mendenhall Glacier
Jet boat tour	One way to get to Glacier Bay

Detour # 3: Misty Fjords

On your way home from Ketchikan, be sure and travel the Misty Fjords.

We made the big loop. Keep in mind, the term misty is a marketing term for rain. If it is raining hard you will not see anything. We entered **Belm Canal** and anchored at **Naha Bay** near **Loring**. We then made the big loop around **Revillagigedo Island** to **Fitzgibbon Cove**. From there we went to Manzanita Bay, which is a much better anchorage than anywhere in Punchbowl Cove. The scenery in **Rudyard Bay** is spectacular if you can nail a sunny day; but the evening winds are abrupt and hard to believe and the anchorage is crowded and deep. Check out **Punchbowl** and then cross over to **Manzanita Bay** for a peaceful night's sleep.

Another spectacular way to see Misty Fjords is by air from Ketchikan. Only do the trip if it is sunny!

http://www.Mistyfjordsair.com

Eddystone Rock is the famous landmark exiting Misty Fjords.

Eddystone Rock

Section Five: Stories

Runaway Girl

1. How to buy a boat and what can happen when you do

No one in his or her right mind buys a boat.

I had never intended to buy a boat. You have to be tricked into it somehow.

Brian called me up one day and asked if I would help him look for a J/30. I said sure, and off we went to Shilshoe Marina. Brian found a J/30. Next-door was a rather large once proud boat that had fallen a bit. Her varnish was peeling; her deck paint was an off grey. But she had a huge proud spar, tough looking rigging, massive winches everywhere and a nearly flush deck. I said to Brian," LOOK AT THAT BEAUTIFUL BOAT!"

Funny how adventures begin –

Brian looked at me, pointed at the boat and said "That boat is way too large. She looks like hell; she needs a lot of work. She's way too much boat. Look at that mast, it's way too tall. She's an old race boat gone to pasture; a fast dog that has run out of the money."

I thought about what he said. At least for a second or two – I looked at him, looked at the boat.

"Underneath that funk beats a proud heart."

Things got a little heated...

"Are you out of your mind? We came here to look at a J/30. There's no way I am going to buy that boat."

"I know you're not going to buy it. It would be wrong for you. It's not a first boat. She's not a beginner boat. She's an Arabian."

Brian was looking a bit concerned. "Now I know you're out of your gourd. Arabian? ... This is not a horse race you moron. That's an old race boat that someone is probably getting a divorce over."

"Mark my words Brian – I am going to buy her."

Brian threw up his hands, "I can't take you anywhere. This was supposed to be my shopping adventure."

What could I say but "The answer seems pretty obvious. Hells Bells, let's buy them both."

Brian didn't give up though, good thing, someone needs to have some common sense. "That boat needs a hell of a lot of work. You'd be insane to buy it."

Oh no. I couldn't let those words go unchallenged. "Maybe it would be insane to buy her, but don't offend her. Of course no friend of mine could have that much common sense. "Well..." Brian said, "She is pretty. Underneath all that she's got some really fine lines. I bet she's a fine sailing boat. But she's not exactly a cruise boat so what would you do with her?"

No hesitation now for me. "Why I'd sail her Up the Inside Passage to Alaska. I've been too long without a boat. Here we are in the finest sailing area in the world, and I've been 6 years stuck on land. I'm sure I could count on a few of the boys from work to sail."

Brian wasn't stupid "More like work on her you mean."

But I knew the answer "Work and then sail. "

There was one more card Brian could play and it was a big one, "Mary will never go for it."

Oops. He had a point. But I regrouped. "Maybe she will. After all she picked me out and I'm a bit like this boat."

Now Brian was intrigued. "How do you figure that?"

I had to find the right words. "I'm not a young quarter horse myself and yet… You don't really think men pick women do you? Women pick men. Since the beginning of time, Women pick men. And boats pick sailors."

And so it came to pass. We bought both boats. The salesman said Star Rover had raced the Maui Race and placed sixth. She was named Saturday's Child at that time. She's cutter rigged, weighs in at about 29,000 lbs., and has 13.5 foot beam. Her mast sands about 70 feet off the water. She has a north main, 4 headsails, 2 chutes, and a spinnaker pole about 12 feet long. She has a roller furling Harken headsail. She is quite traditional, with her aft cockpit, dodger, and chart table and galley just down the ladder. She had an old Isuzu diesel.

Right from the start, she sailed fabulously. She would go to weather at 8 or 9 knots with the best of them. Give her an 18-knot breeze and she sails the pants off nearly all comers. She still has that air of an Arabian about her.

I remember one time sailing in Desolation Sound. We had the 130 Genoa rolled out about half way and we were loafing along. Now I must confess, we have been known to travel with a bit of stuff. Well, truth be told, probably too much stuff. Just then we had on deck 2 kayaks, a mountain bike padlocked to the starboard guardrail, 6 red jerry cans for water and 6 yellow jerry cans for diesel. Not done yet, we had a Yankee trysail strapped on to the cutter stay lashed onto the mast, a 5 horse Evinrude outboard motor mounted on the back rail, a huge spool of rope for stern tie-off lashed to the aft railing, and, of course we had our Avon dinghy lashed to the deck just forward of the dodger.

Anyway, we were sailing merrily along, playing rock and roll, drinking our Beck's beers with the Barbie fired up doing some dogs. That is to say, we were doing our usual bit..., behind us comes up a brand new 40' racing yacht. White sails, all the chaps in uniforms and here she comes after Star Rover. She definitely is going to give us a go. Now the wind was blowing about 20 knots and she was hauling up on us.

We rolled out the 130. Star Rover began to shake her head, like a dog shaking off a coat of snow and stretching out. She began to accelerate. Suddenly the fancy boat behind us began to lose headway. Now the captain on the fancy boat started shouting orders.

On Star Rover Brian flipped over the dogs, and changed the music to faster and louder rock and roll. Over the music we could hear the Captain of his new boat shouting, "Look at that damn boat. Look at all the crap they have on the decks. There is sh**t everywhere. Trim the Genoa in. Damn it. Look at that. She's pulling away from us. Damn it what is the matter with you boys? We can't let that old boat beat us out!"

I am sure the guy went home, poured himself a stiff Scotch, yelled at his dog and blamed his wife.

Whenever we are with some old salts, they ask who made Star Rover. I tell them she is a Miller 44.

They nod, "I know that boat! I chased that damn boat all over the bay. Never could catch her. All we ever saw of her was her transom."

2: The Princess Louisa and her Dragon

Up Agamemnon Channel and off to the east is a little piece of magic called Princess Louisa. Tucked into the mountains hidden from all Crusaders, it's a narrow inland salt lake guarded by an almost invisible dragon moat called Malibu Rapids. Malibu has thrown many crusaders onto the rocks who have come on a quest to see the Princess.

Of course Brian and I had to go and, of course, we had to learn the hard way how to face and tame the dragon.

It was the usual nice day, with good music blasting on the stereo. The beer was cold and the wind was light. The conversation was not quite so laid back ...

Brian's head popped up out of the hatch. "What do you mean we don't have the chart? How can we not have the chart?"

'What do you mean? What do you mean?" was the best I could come up with since I just had told him we didn't have the chart.

Brian wasn't having it though. "How can we not have the chart?!!!"

"Well ..." I said, "... it appears we have two charts of Pender and no charts of the Princess Louisa Inlet. But, we have this book of charts. See. I'm sure there's something in this book. How hard can it be? It's just one big fjord? Famous last words...

Waving the book at me and pointing at a page, Brian asked, not very politely I must say, "What does it say right here in big letters? Very BIG letters – "

Okay. I had to concede that it may have said something like NOT FOR NAVIGATION. But I argued that it was just some sort of copyright malarkey. It doesn't mean you can't use them. I mean we paid sixty-five dollars for the darn book. It didn't say anything like not for navigation on the price tag. No sir. We're talking good old U S of A dollars here.

Since Brian was either praying or cursing I figured I would tell him an old sailor story to cheer him up.

"Look Brian, I once sailed with a guy who used National Geographic for his maps. We were down by the Panama Canal near Punta Mala. He would sail off ahead of me and damned if he didn't get into each harbor ahead of me anchored in the best location. He was the best damn sailor I ever saw."

Brian wasn't buying it and I was none too pleased myself at not having the charts. Charts are in the DO NOT LEAVE HOME WITHOUT THEM category. Charts are the difference between a nice harbor and a great sunset or a frantic MAYDAY followed by lunch in the dinghy.

Still looking at the Not for Navigation charts Brian pointed out that there was no compass rose on them. None – Nada – Nope. He took this rather personally I thought so I told him not to worry, it didn't mean anything; just get the course off the computer. It's a fjord. We just go upstream. We can use the GPS for our compass rose.

"You tricked me into this trip" Brian hollered up at me.

"Did not" I hollered right back.

"Did too – "

"Nope – you wanted to come."

"Sure. I wanted to come until I figured out you're nuts." Brian had hit his stride. " – at least when I DIE my wife and children will get the life insurance I increased for this trip."

We glared at each other, looked at the chart book, looked at each other and started laughing. Okay. Not what you should do. Not what we'd advise anyone cruising to the Princess to do but we were here and we were going.

"Okay Brian, now where are we?" "Right next to that rock ahead of us – " "That's an island Brian. See it's on the chart. An island "

Brian went below to get the book describing Princess Louisa and the Malibu Rapids and to fire up the computer to check the slack tide.

What Brian saw was slack at 3:00 PM. At 6 knots we'd be there by 2:00 PM with time for a leisurely lunch. Knowing that I wasn't the type to sit around having lunch when you're that close to "home" for the night, Brian wondered why we weren't just going through. I told him to check the current.

"Jesus wept! 8 knots – "

Yep. The Princess' dragon, Malibu Rapids, was 30 feet wide at best and moving at 8 knots. We were headed for it. And so Brian took the wheel, I put on a new CD, and brought us some beers. As Brian noted you could summarize our trips in those few words – wheel, music, and beer.

On any quest to face a dragon we all know you first have to find the dragon. About 3 hours later after cruising along, chatting, chugging, enjoying the sun, we spotted a bunch of boats next to a big fancy house. Back to cruising and relaxing until some 30 minutes later I looked up and there was no more channel. I asked Brian where he thought we were allowing as how we were at the END OF THE CHANNEL. Brian looked around and then, wisely I thought, muttered "Bummer" as he turned the boat around. Mutter. Mutter. Fancy house – Rapids – Mutter, Mutter, Mutter.

..... 20 minutes later ....

Robb: "Alright, according to the GPS the channel is to port."

Brian: "I can't see any channel. Here you look."

Robb: "There's a buoy. That has got to be it."

Brian: "Hey! A boat just popped out of there. Well the good news is now we only have to wait 30 minutes for slack tide."

Robb: "Jesus Christ I cannot believe that is the channel. "

Brian: "There's another boat coming out!"

Robb: "That's it. That's Malibu Rapids. It's slack tide. Let's go in."

Brian decided I should take the wheel and so I took over and sent him to the bow as our lookout. When I grabbed my life vest and put it on Brian got a bit concerned. "You must be really paranoid" was his comment followed by his tracking down and putting on *his* life vest.

The conversation got short and to the point really fast ...

Robb: "Remember the signals... two arms over head means go straight. And face backwards when you talk."

Brian: "What?"

Robb: "Face backwards Brian when you want to talk. Backwards."

Brian: "Okay but boy it looks pretty hairy."

By then we were on our way and I was wide-eyed and getting more wide-eyed. "Jesus! It's not very wide – according to the book it's a big S. Looks like we got a 4 knot current coming out."

Brian was getting distracted. "Hey look there are some boats coming up behind us." With a touch of irritation I responded – just a touch – "Just look ahead. See anything?"

Brian: "Yes – I see it's pretty damn narrow."

He had that right and then some. Not only was it a trite slim, to say the least, but ... "Jesus Christ, there's a lot of current. This damn channel can't be 30 feet wide."

Still taking it all in Brian pointed out all the people on the deck of the big house. They were watching the show no doubt. But then Brian spotted our first crisis ... "Hey! There's a boat coming out...turn to starboard! Turn!"

"We can't turn. If we try and turn we're going to corkscrew and wind up on the rocks. We aren't turning."

Brian had his eyes peeled front and on the boat coming at us: "Here he comes. He isn't turning either."

Shouting back "I think we can slide over a little..." I tweaked the wheel and we passed each other with about 6 inches between us. The closest I've ever been to a 40-foot aluminum powerboat with a 200 h.p. outboard. The closest I ever want to be – even standing still. The powerboat passengers waved to us as they blinked by. Waved. Wow.

Brian felt obliged to point out that they were "Friendly folks". I demurred. Then ...

..... Wham ...... The boat hit a log.

Immediately followed by Brian calling out, "Watch out for the log." My reply wasn't friendly, "We just hit the son of a bitch." Brian pointed out the obvious, "I know we hit it! I couldn't see it," and I had to concede, "I know I know. That's alright ... she's a tough boat. "

"You're pretty calm" was Brian's next comment but I had to tell him the truth, "My mouth is just too dry to speak." I barely got the words shouted out when ....

.... Our next crisis was on us .....

Brian: "Look out for that speedboat." The eternal optimist that I am replied, "It's no big deal. I'm sure he sees us."

Brian pointed out how wrong I was, "The kid waterskiing just fell in!!!! Right in front of us – GO TO NEUTRAL. Now. Neutral."

As I slammed Star Rover into reverse, "Mother of God! Can't they see us? Don't they know we can't stop on a dime?" I spun the wheel to starboard and whispered, "Father who art in Heaven."

Brian called out, "That's it. We've missed him. We're clear. We made it through."

My words were from the heart, "Please take the wheel Brian. I'm going down for a beer, a breather, and then I need to pull up the floorboards and see if we're taking on any water."

The beer tasted great. We hadn't taken on any water. And we had faced the dragon guarding the Princess. Malibu Rapids had allowed us through.

When I returned to deck I knew why sailboats braved the rapids. The inlet was (and is) a magical place. We'd brought Star Rover into a mountain lake. ... "Look at those mountains Brian. Check out the snow. My God this is fabulous. I don't think I've seen many places more beautiful than this."

Brian steered us towards the falls and we cruised up the fjord to the lovely Chatterbox Waterfall. He'd checked the book and it said to anchor at the dock but the dock was full.

We sauntered up next to a fancy looking powerboat rafted to another powerboat near the end of the dock. We asked if we could tie-up to them but they had been told that you could only raft up to a max of 3 wide and they were the fourth already.

Checking out the scene Brian decided to take the dinghy and go over to the dock and talk to the ranger. Sounded like a great plan to me. I idled and looked around. There were about 20 boats on the outside of the dock and 15 on the inside. Definitely a crowded dock but it was such a lovely spot I didn't mind just waiting.

When Brian got back he brought a wealth of news,

"Hey, I found out a lot. First of all that couple on the nice sailboat is stuck up. The ranger doesn't have much to say except we have to get permission from another boat before we dock next to them.

But the nicest guy is on a small sailboat called Rumb Line. He says the way to tell the slack is to use Port Atkinson and add ½ hour. We were about an hour early. Turns out there's an inside slack listed on Nobeltec that's wrong by about an hour. We were an hour early and that is why we had so much current. Also he said we were nuts to go through at low slack."

Only reply possible was, "No sh** Sherlock. But good to know for next time."

Continuing with what he'd learned Brian had the anchoring info we needed, "But the good news is he says there's a perfect anchorage over by that small waterfall around the bend. Apparently there are metal rings at high tide banged into the rocks all the way along the bank. You drop the hook in 150 feet of water and just back over to the cliff. Then you tie onto a ring and let yourself out back out maybe 50 feet."

Sounded like a plan to me since the dock *was* really crowded and it would be great to be away from any "stuck-up yachts" and be off by ourselves. We motored over towards the third waterfall and saw a lovely 44-foot Krogan motor yacht. The couple came out on deck and we got a welcome and the details we needed on depth and anchor dragging from them..."Hi! It's about 80 feet here and we've got out 200 feet of chain. If you're thinking of right in front of the waterfall it would probably be a perfect spot."

We motored over until we were just below a spectacular waterfall. The fish finder was 40 feet near the falls, 120 feet further out. We let out all our chain and I took the dinghy over to a tree right by the falls. Everyone said to tie the stern line to a metal ring, but I couldn't find the ring so I tied our aft line to the tree. I got back to Star Rover and we let out the aft line until we were 50 feet from the falls. Worked great.

When you looked up out of the cockpit hatch all you could see was the rush of falling water. The breeze from the waterfall cooled the boat. Once we killed the motor you could hear perfect music – the sound of falling water. Everywhere mountains rose up from the fjord and around the point Chatterbox crashed and roared.

"Well Brian, I think this is as good as it gets. We're not going to find any place any nicer than this. It's free, we can't spend one penny, and we can stay a month."

Ever wise Brian replied, "Or until we run out of beer."

3. Fjordland and the Parrot's Beak

As soon as you make the turn into Kynoch Inlet you see a huge splash of white. Sea Mist headed right for it and Star Rover followed. We'd been traveling together for a while and enjoying each other's company – good folks. Now we were ready for Fjordland.

As you approach, the falls loom large. The noise is huge; we slip into a magical world. There are no other boats, no noise, just the roar of the mighty falls. Sea Mist goes closer and closer until she's right up front. We click a picture and then we simply put the camera down. It's almost as if this part of the world is so sacred we are afraid to disturb it. We've wandered into the land of Carlos Castaneda; we simply stand and stare in awe.

We turn and head up the Channel. It's hard to pull away and as we motor on the falls become smaller and smaller.

We jump back through that post card portal into the ordinary world again. We come up into another canyon. We pass a wall of granite that looks like Half Dome. We begin to feel smaller and smaller as the walls on either side tower above us.

Gerard had asked me at the beginning of the trip where we were going. Here it is, I thought. This is our destination. This is the Inside Passage at its best.

We move slowly up the Channel. Gerard takes it all in and reflects aloud. ....

"I always wanted to travel the Northwest Inside Passage. Now that we're here I can say I am truly thankful. Look at that crack in the cliff. What could have caused that? Lightning – earthquake – water and time? How splendid. No development, no boats, no planes. There's nothing here but our tiny boats. I wonder how old this magnificent granite face is? Who were the first men to look at this valley? Did they travel in their canoes and see it just as we are now? Could they have failed to see it with the same wonder we're experiencing?"

We come up to the end of the fjord and it's time to find a place to anchor. Sea Mist goes over towards the shore. She turns sharply as we see the color of the bottom change. There's a small anchorage between the deep water we are in and the shallow water near shore. The wind is blowing up thirty knots and good thing you can't see the future because even though it all goes well for a while things are about to get really, really scary and really strange.

"Star Rover. Star Rover. This is Sea Mist. Do you read?"

"Star Rover here"

"Switch to 69. Looks to be a pretty tight spot. And watch out! We're showing 20 feet right behind us. We're anchored in 60 feet with 300 feet of chain out. We're holding. I think you can come up alongside."

On Star Rover I wasn't as sure, "It's blowing a bit. Do you think I can anchor inside of you?" "Not really. I think it would be better if you tied up alongside."

That had some advantages but, "I'm worried your anchor won't hold both boats. I've got a hell of a lot of windage with this 70-foot mast. Maybe I could drop an anchor out here and back in toward you." We agree on this approach and I start working to come up alongside him.

We come in on the cliff side and turn up next to Sea Mist. There's about 10 feet separating the boats. Gerard throws the line over to Sea Mist, but the line goes over the top of the lifeline instead of through the bottom. Yikes. I'm yelling over at Ron. "Hells Bells, this is not working. Let go the line." The boats are bouncing around in the 30-knot wind and we veer off narrowly missing scraping the side of Ron's boat.

I head out into deeper water again. Now I'm sweating a bit more. I'm looking at the chart trying to find another anchorage. I'm thinking of heading back out and I'm fretting big time – I wish I had 400 feet of high test 5/8 chain instead of 300 feet of 3/8 BBB chain.

Back to the radio.

"I don't know Ron. This is kind of hairy! I damn near scratched your boat and I know how long you worked building her. I want no part of being the first one to scratch her."

Testimony to how powerboats and sailboats really do get along Ron replies, "You'll be fine. Just try again."

Still not convinced, "Maybe we'll take Star Rover out of here. The wind is strong. The beach is shallow and damn close behind you. You really think your anchor will hold both our boats?"

Ron's confidant I'm sure. The wind will die down towards evening and Karol is making a pot roast dinner. Give it another shot."

The pot roast may have been the deciding factor. "Okay. We'll go for it but I have to say this makes me uneasy. When I come around the wind wants to blow the mast off. What the hell."

We go around. This time the line goes right over and we're both putting out more and more bumpers to cushion the meet. Star Rover comes up alongside and lies off perfectly with one foot or so between the boats. I heave a great sigh of relief. So far, so good.

Ron's a boat man I trust and so I when he suggests we go out and drop our anchor in a V towards the point I get ready to do just that.

Our "dinghy" for the trip is a collapsible, unsinkable boat we've named Uncle Wiggly. We'll take Wiggly out, drop the other anchor, and then we'll deploy the stern anchor. Now that we're tied alongside Sea Mist I'd just as soon stay there.

Ron offers to help but we've got it. It will just take a while to put Uncle Wiggly together and rig the anchors. We have a 60-pound Bruce and 100 feet of chain and 200 feet of anchor rode. It's a good beefy anchor and I'm sure it will hold fine.

When Uncle Wiggly is ready we put the outboard engine on the back. Naturally, we don't have the gate on the side we need – does anyone ever have the gate on the side they need? I have to crawl under the life rails and so it takes longer and I have more trouble getting in and out of the boat.

Then I have to go into the front bunk and pull out the Bruce. I put together the chain and the anchor. It is a hawking big anchor for the little boat and I am already fretting over how to get the chain over without swamping the boat. We finally get in. I'm thinking pot roast though so I just keep on working.

We grab our life vests at the last minute. I put on the inflatable and Gerard puts on the blue vest. We fire up the outboard motor and head out, letting out anchor line as we go.

Ron is on the front of his boat giving us hand signals none of which we understand. He's putting both hands together over his head and motioning away from the boat. I guess he means go out further. Every time we get the line ready to drop, Ron points us in another direction or we start to drift back too close to the boat.

Finally, we seem to be in about the right spot and I start lowering the chain over the side. The chain is mighty damn heavy and the boat starts to lurch to the side – the chain is pulling the boat down so we have very little freeboard. I get nervous and give the anchor a last minute flip over the side. Wiggly now only has 1 inch of freeboard. I throw the anchor overboard but ...

... the fluke catches on the back corner of Wiggly. I am horrified, not even breathing, wondering what to do, and watching the color drain from Gerard's face just as it's probably gone from mine. If I move we're going over and ...

... just at that moment a wave comes over the transom of the boat and fills it with water. Over we go. #&%!!#

Two seconds later we're in the water. The boat is completely submerged except for a small snout – a little curved hook barely above the surface which looks just like the beak of a parrot.

A ways off, the gas tank is, bobbing up and down like the float on a crab pot. I look over at Gerard and tell him what we both already know, "Swim. Swim for Star Rover. Swim like you're going to freeze to death, which we will in about 15 minutes."

"&%^&## Wiggly. Unsinkable my ass "

Gerard and I start swimming frantically for the boat. I don't inflate my life vest and I'm making good progress. Gerard seems to be having a bit of trouble because the vest is floating up around his neck but undaunted he rolls over on his back and strikes out.

I look up and there's Ron and Karol ... horrified looks on their faces, rushing to launch their dingy, and frantic because the crane isn't set.

Ron's shouting, "Are you guys alright?" I check Gerard and he's coming along and I'm making progress. I take the time to shout back. "Fine. We're fine. We're just taking a little swim in the freezing cold water to boost our spirits."

Gerard is still a ways off and I wonder if I should wait for him, or get out of the water. It's cold. Really COLD and I decide better to get out of the water and get ready to get back in if Gerard needs some help. Got to move fast though so I pull the swim ladder on Star Rover's transom down, get on board and get some dry clothes. I can dive in again if I need to. I'm shivering but as soon as I get out of the water and get my shirt off I'm OK. And Gerard is getting close.

Meanwhile the rescue dinghy is having its own issues. Ron and Karol have their boat launched but the motor won't start. He's pulling the cord but he'd run the gas out to protect the motor. Finally it starts.

Gerard makes it to the ladder and comes up. We're both safe and in dry clothes and we're feeling really amazed and grateful.

Once convinced all's good I look at the parrot's beak and start doing the math. Wiggly is still a parrot's beak with the rest below water, the motor is a 1000 bucks and probably gone. Then there's 700 bucks for the anchor – probably gone. Add in the tools in the bottom of the boat, crescent wrench, pliers and my favorite vice grips – probably gone. No sign of the oars – probably gone. 2000 bucks for the outboard – gone for sure ...

S***! I look over at Ron and he is obviously really relived that we're okay. He can't know I'm fretting about lost money. Can't I just be happy we are alive? And ...

I am happy. I am happy. Well actually, I'm shivering and could swear I hear a parrot squawking.

Gerard asks if he should come with us to get the sunken unsinkable Uncle Wiggly. No. I ask him to wait on board and help with pulling Wiggly back upright.

Ron and I set off in his Avon. I'm reminded how stable the Avon is for things like throwing over the anchor. Stable like Wiggly wasn't. Mutter. Mutter. We motor over to the Parrot's Beak.

I lean over and ... BEHOLD ... the anchor line has one turn around the seat. It's holding on by a hair's breadth. I curse myself for not attaching a bumper float to the line but ... oh well, what am I doing whining. No time for that. The anchor is saved. I grab the rope. We take the line over to Star Rover and it streams behind us. Gerard has the boat hook out. We wrap the line around the hook and he pulls it in. Nine hundred dollars up. Praise the Lord.

Now we go back out to Wiggly. I'm thinking we need to tow Uncle Wiggly onto the beach and maybe we then right her. I'm also thinking I can hear the parrot squawking, *come get me, come get me.* Maybe I'd had a few too many minutes in the water.

We get to Wiggly and grab her painter and then head back to Star Rover. Wiggly begins to act like giant sea slug. As we get even with Star Rover she refuses to move. Ron is revving up the nine-horse motor higher and higher. We seem to be going nowhere and the parrot isn't saying anything.

Just then I notice the swim ladder is still down from when Gerard and I got back on board. As we go around the stern of the boat there's a danger that Wiggly will get punctured on the ladder. I'm yelling at Gerard to pull up the swim ladder, he's reaching for it with the boat hook and just at that moment ...

Wiggly seems to break free and race toward the back of Star Rover. Of course Uncle Wiggly, with no sense of self-preservation and despondent from sinking, is going to commit suicide on the swim ladder.

Wham. Wiggly smashes into swim ladder. Ouch. Another moment of good-bye Wiggly and then .... Instead of catching on the ladder, the ladder hits Wiggly and miraculously she rights herself. Suddenly Wiggly turns upright and comes to a dead stop. The Outboard motor is still attached! Praise to the Baby Jesus.

Wiggly is floating three quarters full of water – proud and upright – unsinkable as advertised. Mother of God it's a miracle. The motor is still on the back. The tools are still in the bottom. The oars are attached.

All of us stand there dumbfounded. No one can even think of anything to say for the next few minutes. Speechless. Outboard. Tools. Oars. Wiggly. It's all there. And I could swear I could hear the parrot squawking *told you so, told you.*

Finally Karol says with a smile, "I bet you weren't even thinking about the money. And how about some pot roast!"

Later, I ask Ron to sign an affidavit as to the wonder of God. To the beak. To the resurface. To the swim ladder collision and all the stuff. He did. I still have it.

Though Wiggly did come through for me I decided I needed a regular ruby dinghy and a postscript ...

Wiggly's next owner is a dentist. When he came to look at her he began the conversation by saying he knew a lot about these boats, and that they were … Unsinkable ….

You betcha!

He hasn't said anything about parrots but he's happy.

The tools still work and the motor still runs five years later. After a year of living on the back of the boat, she started on the third pull.

Some guys have all the luck.

And I'm very happy with our new rubber boat with the big floats on the side. The new boat is hard to row but the funny thing is … no one says anything about it and there's no hint of a parrot anywhere.

HOOPED
OR CAPTAIN GEORGE VANCOUVER HAS NO MOTOR AND BRAVES THE CANYON OF DEATH!

It's not my fault. Isn't that what everyone says? Of course it was. Doesn't mean I can't snivel and whine a bit before starting on this chapter.

It is weird to thank someone who has traveled so many ocean miles could be tense over a little passage across the Strait of Georgia, but lets face it , we have gotten the snot beat out of us in that little nasty bit of water called the Straight of Georgia. It is something about the darn wind against the tide, or the shallow water or something. Anyway the wind comes up in the afternoon and if you are not careful you get beat up.

We did the right thing, up at 5;00 am. You have to get and out in the calm of dawn..

Whisky Zulu is open.so. .all is good.

It is beautiful morning, clear and cold, a slight zephyr from the south. Perfect. Forecast was for increasing winds to 20 knots in the afternoon. No problem. By afternoon with any luck we would be in Pender in a safe harbor.

Anchor up. Off we go out of Shelter Island and north towards the ferry dock. Off we go north around the island. Thank heavens there is no smoke coming out of the ferries at the dock so we wont be run over... all is good. The main is up with one reef . contrary to popular belief, it is lovely. The main keeps the boat steady and the motor pushes us along at 8 knots

By seven we are half way across the channel. We turn off the motor and roll out the full 150 genoa with 800 square feet of pulling power. We shake the reef out.. and are gusting to a lovely 8 knots in light winds.

We crank the music up and break out the first beer. I know it is a tad early. But it is the Straits of Georgia, which everyone knows can be a pain. We drop into a mild coma…… oops we better switch over to the weather channel .

the revised weather forecast.

"Revised weather forecast for in the Strait of Georgia north of Nanaimo: Gale force warning in effect winds increasing to 30 knots."

Crap not again. Seems like every time we come out here , we get pounded .here comes the first gust. Star Rover starts to pick up speed. 5 knots, six knots, seven knots. We turn the engine off. Still seven knots a. the wind builds.

The strange thing about this boat I she loves to go fast. Now we are doing eight knots now nine knots.. Now she is starting to buck and rock and roll.

Prudence?

Speed?

What if something breaks?

She is not a spring colt any more. We roll in the genoa a bit.

Now the waves are building. They are tall with a short fetch. Water starts blasting off the bow and into the cockpit. Jesus it is cold. I can't let go of the wheel (This was before we had an auto pilot.)

I look up the channel and see the worst sight, a tug pulling a log boom. Drats it is coming down right where we want to go.

For just a minute I think about going in front of it. Dumb idea. A picture of the cable slicing through Star Rover flashes through my brain. O.K.so we will go behind it. We turn north to let it get ahead of us. Bam a gust of wind knocks the boat over 20 degrees. Bam another blast. Now the water starts kicking up. Crap. I think about pulling another reef> in the main. Now the wind lets up a bit. It's not that bad. STAY THE COURSE. Stay in the cockpit. Brace up. Star rover accelerates 8 knots ,9knotts , and 10 knots. Must be the current pushing us. The Genoa line starts to creak. Crap. I have to do something soon. We are just behind the log boom. Suddenly BAM. BAM. Crunch. BAM another hit along the hull suddenly the prop goes bang. The boat starts to wobble. I slow the engine to idle. We are still vibrating a bit but not so bad. We have hit a log and it has scrapped under the boat dinging the prop. I tear down below and pull up the floorboards. No water coming in. thank God. One thing about Star Rover, the bilge is flat and only 4 or so inches separate the bottom of the boat from the floorboards so if there really is a problem water would be over the floor. I go aback up and roll in the Genoa.

Crap where is the nearest place to haul out? I think frantically. LUND. We are not that far from Lund maybe only 10 miles. We turn and headsouth.40 minutes later we sail into the small cove behind Lund . We come up to a dock and see a huge contraption parked by the water. I tie the boat up at the dock and go up the hill to a small trailer and knock on the door. There are probably 30 boats up on the flat. I go inside and meet a woman. Hi she says I'm Jerry. Hi many people I say I'm robb and Star Rover and I have gotten ourselves into a bit of a situation.

She looks over at me. You mean hit a log and you need to haul your boat in a hurry.

How did you figure that. I said

Not that many people run up the hill. She shows me her video camera. On it some silly man is running up the hill with his bright red yacht jacked unbuttoned and a life preserver hanging from his neck.

That would be me. And yes.

You didn't happen to go behind a log boom in this weather did you?

I thought the logs were all tied together.

They are not. Only the perimeter is tied and when it blows up they start pitching logs like the New York Mets.

Any chance you could pull me out today? Like maybe right now?

Mister you are in luck the tide is high. Luckily the rig is down side already.t be

That wouldn't be that big yellow contraption that looks kind of Mad Max made would it? Can it handle 28000 lbs.?

And then some. I outta know. We built it.

Can you motor your boat over?

I can but it is a little iffy diffy. I might have winged the prop.

No problems I will just use the launch and bring a line over to you.

He gets on the radio. Fire up the loader. We got a live one.

I go back to Star Rover, I see a Huge Earth mover start down the hill and I follow it. Jerry comes down in a pickup. She fires up the huge contraption by the dock. It looks like some kind of Transformer from the logging business.

We get the boat over and Jerry drives the monster out over Star Rover. Diesels and puffing cables are whirling. Things are squeaking and the sling begins to lower. Little by little Jerry pulls up the boat with nary a scratch. The huge crane machine takes the load with no problem. Now she drives out over the land and hooks the huge beast with Star Rover hanging to the monster loader.

We can't make it up the hill with this much weight so we use the loader for a bit more traction, she says.

Up we go.

Insert picture.

Jerry sets star rover down in the large clearing at the top. Someone has put a lot of gravel down but the chunks are the size of baseballs. I have a bit of trouble walking.

Asks " Do you need power. Yes I say. I see a box of electrical rising out of the stones surrounded by water with four or five electrical courts running through it.

Boy Howdy.

Jerry climbs down out of the monster transporter and ambles over. We look at the gash in the front of the boat and the winged prop. Do you need us to contract anyone to fix the fiberglass and the prop?

No I say : I can fix it myself but I probably need help pulling off the prop.

She drives off.

I am sitting on the ground staring up 13 feet at the boat.

A truck drives up and a guy gets out with a bunch of stands to prop up the hull.

He talks. I have a bit of trouble understanding him. Then I realize he has a hearing impediment and he speaks a bit funny but he can read my lips.

Can we set her on her keel? He asks

It sounds like

Ken wesetther onher KEEEIIIIL?

I say yes. I ask him if he can pull the prop off. He nods.

He sets the boat down expertly on several 12 by 12s. and proceeds to place the stands.

He comes back ½ hour later with a welding torche.He fires it up and begins heating the prop with the torch. I look at him funny. He turns off the torch and loosens the nuts holding on the prop. He hits the prop once with a bronze sludge hammer from the front side. It pops off.

THEERZE MOOR TAN ONE whey to SKION a CAT.

I look at him. There is more than one way to skin a cat.

THAZ WHAT I SWAID. He laughs. I laugh. I like this guy.

The Canadian people say they can special order a prop and get it for 870 dollars in five days.

Over the course of the next few days I call my wife and have here drive down to Tacoma Prop and pick up a new 1812LH prop for 480 bucks.

She drives up and I put on the new prop. I have by now repaired the hull. Repainted the boat . I am ready to leave. I loo

The mechanic drives by in his pick up. He says

YOUUS SHOUUD repllllaiiice the shaft..with a NEWW ONE.

I look at him.

Hell no. Hell no I am out of here. The boat is ready to go now.

He nods and salutes .AS if to say... I was young and in a hurry once...then I learned some sense.

I thank him for pulling the prop.

He nods again and taps the shaft and smiles. Then go hoes over to the crane and drives it over and picks up Star Rover..

Jerry comes over. We should be able to splash you at 4;30 the tide will be high enough.

Great I say. Can't wait to get to sea

Hell no.

Hell no! I am out of here. The boat is ready to go now.

He nods and salutes .AS if to say... I was young and in a hurry once...then I learned some sense.

I thank him for pulling the prop.

He nods again and taps the shaft and smiles. Then goes over to the crane and drives it over and picks up Star Rover..

Jerry comes over. We should be able to splash you at 4;30 the tide will be high enough.

Great I say. Can't wait to get to sea

By 600 Star Rover is back in the water and my wife is getting into her car to go home.

The next morning I fire up the engine and head up the coast to Pender and then Forward Harbor. I pull into Forward Harbor after transiting the four rapids.

FORWARD HARBOR

Morning. There is no one in the harbor. I hear the cry of gulls. Solitude.

I fire up the motor and crank up the anchor. I put the motor in gear to pull the anchor out of the sand. Only I don't go anywhere. NOTHING. I put the boat in reverse.

NOTHING

I put her in forward again

NOTHING.

Crap.

I must have run over a fishing line., but I don't remember seeing any floats.

I put on my rubber top, fins and goggles and jump over the side. I look under the boat. NO PROP

Crap.

I get back up on the boat. And strip off all my gear and go down and look at the shaft from the inside. Everything looks normal.

I think.

I reach for the Scotch. I have a couple of shots. I get up and let down the anchor. Luckily there is no current and no wind.

I start daydreaming.

That can't be right. I have a prop.

I take a few more shots of scotch.

Crap

I put on my gear and jump over again. I look. I see 6 inches of shaft coming out of the boat and then NOTHING>

CRAP the shaft has broken.

Somehow the new prop is gone. The shaft is gone my 480 dollars is gone. Rover and I are in the middle of nowhere.

I try my cell phone. No signal. I remember we bought a sat phone for just such emergencies. I dial up a towing service.

Hi I am on a sailboat and I am stuck at Forward Harbor. I wonder if you have someone who can tow me to the nearest port, Cambell River.

How much do you weigh ? 28,000 lbs. but she is very easy to tow. Let me call you back

. An hour later, the phone rings. I have found someone to tow you. Because of your weight and distance I have contacted a towboat. Here is the number.

I call. I describe my situation. Yes we can tow you. We can be there in 4 hours.

How much.

Between 6 and 8 thousand dollars.

Silence

Say again

Between 6 and 8 thousand dollars. But your insurance will probably pay for some of it.

Over my dead body-

Crap. Thanks but no thanks.

I call my wife.

Hi honey. Remember that nice shiny prop you bought from Tacoma?

Yes

I may need another one.

That Lund guy said you needed a new shaft

How would he know that? How can you know that from just looking at it?

Experience? Knowledge. Smarts?

And I have...?

Sometimes we are a bit hard headed.

Sweetheart. God gave you a lot of gifts, but patience was not one of them.

Well, I'll call you later. I just have to figure how to get out of here. I look up and a Krogen comes into the harbor and drops her hook near by.

After a decent amount of time, I row over.

Hi there. Lovely spot

Any chance you could give me a tow out past the reef into Suderland Channel?

No problem they say. We will be leaving tomorrow around nine and we can tow out.

I go back to the boat and turn on the weather. The weather in Johnston Straits is a bit of a joke. They always post gale warnings even when the wind is light. But for tomorrow they are predicting light winds from the north. No Warnings.

Next morning The Krogen guys come by and drop a line. I frantically haul up the anchor as we begin to heat out to the entrance. There is a nasty reef just outside the entrance and some strong currents. The wind is light. I do not have the sails up. We head out and round the corner into Sutherland Straits. As we round the corner the wind blows like hell right on the nose.

I'm thinking Oh Crap maybe I can get them to tow me to Campbell River. We clear the corner .I go below to see if the kitchen plates are stowed. I come back up the hatch just as the woman on the Korgan throws the line off the back of their boat and waves. I am too embarrassed to say anything. They steam off.

Crap I don't have the sails up.

No motor.

There is land on three sides of me not ½ a mile away.

SAIL OR DIE.

George Vancouver did it. He didn't have a motor or even charts. Of course he did have longboats with 30 guys in them towing him around. On the other hand he could not go to weather. Say what you will, Star Rover is a smasher to weather. And by god now is the time to prove it. I roll out the Genoa about half way. We pick up speed to 4 knots. We are not headed in exactly the right direction, but at least we will not end up on the rocks. I tie the wheel and frantically begin putting up the main .I get the main up about half way and the wind gusts to 25. I hear the weather.

Gale warnings in the morning, followed by calm in the afternoon.

GREAT

Off we go. Rover knows she is pulling for her life and she sails like the dickens, we tack back and forth, back and forth. We are pinching but edging our 2ay up the channel.

SAIL or DIE.

The sat. phone rings. It is Mary Frances.

 Hi how is it going?

Fine dear, I got a tow from some nice people and now we are sailing up the channel. I think we will sail down to Discovery Marina in Cambell River. I need you to meet me there with another prop, but I have to get hauled out so I will give you a call when I get closer.

So how are you going to get down there?

Sail, what other choice do we have? We are on our way already.

But didn't you say Seymour Narrows was dangerous?

Great she doesn't listen to half of what I say, but one whiff of danger and out comes a mind like a steel trap.

Oh it's exaggerated. It is not that bad.

Besides Star Rover will look after us.

Long as you don't do something stupid...

Capt. Vancouver did it. And Star Rover is a fine boat. She will see us through. Ill call u when I get closer. I frantically look up Seymour Narrows in the guidebook. A

Seymour Narrows is a 5 km (3.1 mi) section of the Discovery Passage in British Columbia known for strong tidal currents. [1] Discovery Passage lies between Vancouver Island at Menzies Bay, British Columbia and Quadra Island except at its northern end where the eastern shoreline is Sonora Island. The section known as Seymour Narrows begins about 18 km (11 mi) from the south end of Discovery Passage where it enters the Georgia Strait near Campbell River. For most of the length of the narrows, the channel is about 750 m wide. Through this narrow channel, currents can reach 15 KN.

Seymour Narrows was described by Captain George Vancouver as "one of the vilest stretches of water in the world."[2] Even after Ripple Rock was removed, it remains a challenging route. In March 1981, the Star Philippine, a freighter ran aground in the narrows.

Seymour Narrows is notable also because the flowing current can be sufficiently turbulent to realize a Reynolds number of about 10^9, i.e.

one billion, which is possibly the largest Reynolds number regularly attained in natural water channels on Earth (the current speed is about 8 m/s, the nominal depth about 100 m). Turbulence develops usually around a Reynolds number of 2000, depending on the geometric structure of the channel. Thank Heavens; I am not real up on by Reynolds numbers.

I frantically study the chart for places to anchor while we wait for the right tide. I come up with Discovery Channel and Blind Bay. The bay looks good but a bit small. I wonder about anchoring under sail. The currents are fierce. Is it better to go with the tide or try for slack?

Down we go to Blind Bay and we make flying stop anchor.

I furl the Genoa.

 Wow first leg completed. Now we study the currents. The next morning there is not much wind but the tide is just beginning to ebb. The max current is 12 knots in Race passage. What the hell let's do it? Out we go and right away the boat is caught in the current and starts to take off. We can tack back and forth to slow down and try to hit the center of the Race channel. We are going about 4 knots. As the day progresses so does our speed 5,6,7,8. Down we go. Oh boy. Five hours later we are near Seymour Narrows. I look through the binoculars and see a standing wave at the bottom about 3 feet high. How bad can it be? Now I am thinking of crap how do I stop this thing. I turn around and sail up current. That is even freakier. I turn back around. Here we go. Speed builds up 8, 9, 10, and now 11. Now there are waves and bumps and whirlpools and rip tides. Oh dear. Perhaps this was not the most prudent choice. Perhaps I should have gone at slack like all the books say. But then I would have been trapped at the bottom where all the riptides can get hold of you.

Where's your sense of adventure? Dear Baby Jesus if we make it through this one I promise to be more prudent, *way more prudent* in the future....

We bomb through the narrows and hit the standing wave at about 12 to 14 knots. Our bow rises and then drops about 3 feet. Hoops a dozy. Bam we are through. Now we see all kinds of cross currents and ripples and swirls. The wind comes up a bit to 10 knots. We have steerage. Wahoo. We made it. We float on down to just outside of the marina. I get on the radio. I talk to a chirpy young woman. Just come right on in to slip C30 it is a starboard tie. Great I say. I am thinking Star Rover is under full sail. We should only take out two or three boats when we land. I look over and see a 40 ft. powerboat named Pilgrims Progress. I think the name sounds friendly and I hail them on Channel 16.

This is Star Rover. We seemed to have lost power I wonder if you could tow us into the Marina.

No problem, Always a pleasure to help another traveler.

Well this Pilgrim thanks you.

They tow us in.

Now to fix the boat: After a week of eating hamburgers and beet and calming down after our harrowing adventure, I find out there is a haul out railroad right across the channel. I talk one of the fancy rubber tourist boats into towing us over to the other side. We get over there and they pull us right up on their railroad. I get out onto land and one of the boatyard fellows comes up. We stare at the 6 inches of shaft protruding from the hull.

He looks at me: Hooped . You are surely hooped.

I had no idea what he meant .

Yep I said. HOOPED. (Hooped is the Canadian equal of SCRE*ED.)

Well he said, I know just the man to mill you up a new shaft.

Great I said.

Do you have a propeller?

I'll have you wife bring one up. She has had lots of practice. She just brought up a new one last week

.

About the Author:

During his third year in college Robb Keystone's roommate got a bit paranoid (it was the 60s) and decided to flee the USA. He'd bought all the materials and plans to build a sailboat but it would take too long. He was leaving by air for Norway in the morning. Everything could be had for six hundred dollars.

Robb paid up instantly, dropped out of college, and built a Brown 42 foot Sea Runner trimaran in one year. He sailed her down to South America from San Francisco, through the Panama Canal, and then up to Florida.

Upon returning to the USA he looked at his resume, checked his wallet, and went off to find a job. But the love affair with boats was in place.

In the years since his first boat Robb's been a beaver wrangler, a contractor, and a builder. Eventually he found his way to Seattle – probably the call of the sailing.

To finance his boats Robb's worked in the computer business building computer infrastructure for Amazon and Zillow. In

About the Author:

During his third year in college Robb Keystone's roommate got a bit paranoid (it was the 60s) and decided to flee the USA. He'd bought all the materials and plans to build a sailboat but it would take too long. He was leaving by air for Norway in the morning. Everything could be had for one dollar.

Robb paid up instantly, dropped out of college, and built a Brown 42 foot Sea Runner trimaran in one year. He sailed her down to South America from San Francisco, through the Panama Canal, and then up to Florida.

Upon returning to the USA he looked at his resume, checked his wallet, and went off to find a job. But the love affair with boats was in place.

In the years since his first boat Robb's been a beaver wrangler, a contractor, and a builder. Eventually he found his way to Seattle – probably the call of the sailing.

To finance his boats Robb's worked in the computer business building computer infrastructure for Amazon and Zillow. In his spare time he found another love – painting and painting scantily clad women especially.

Boats, women, construction – that's his story.

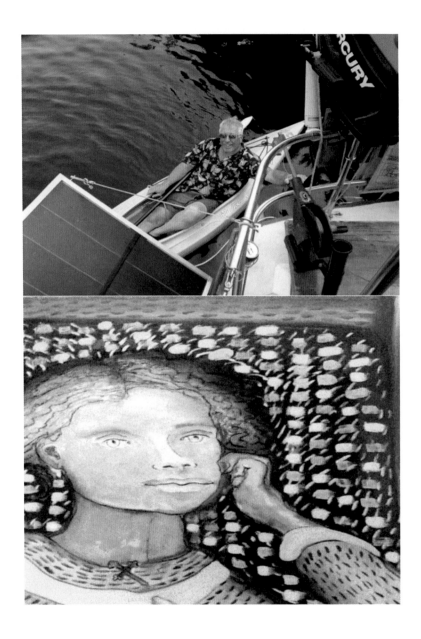

Books:

HERE ARE THE BOOKS WE LIKE:

For Charts:

Evergreen Pacific Exploring- Puget Sound to British Columbia. The only decent compendium-

FOR CURRENTS AND TIDES:
2012 Canadian Tide and Current Tables Volume 5 and I 6

Ports and Passes: Ports and Passes - Tides Currents & Charts 2012

FOR SAILING GUIDES:
 The old standby: Charlie's Charts (Victoria to Glacier Bay, Alaska)

Don Douglas and Reanne Hemingway-Douglas "Exploring the inside passage to Alaska

Dreamspeaker Cruising Guide: The Broughton Islands

Reid Harbor – Glacier Bay Alaska

Index

Thanks to:

Seaview North for getting Rover into shape, and CHAZZZAM Signs & Graphics for the orcas

End

Made in the USA
Las Vegas, NV
19 April 2023

70804912R00095